Writing About Cool

Hypertext and Cultural Studies in the Computer Classroom

Jeff Rice

University of Detroit Mercy

PEARSON
Longman

New York   San Francisco   Boston
London   Toronto   Sydney   Tokyo   Singapore   Madrid
Mexico City   Munich   Paris   Cape Town   Hong Kong   Montreal

Senior Vice President and Publisher: Joseph Opiela
Marketing Manager: Tamara Wederbrand
Production Manager: Douglas Bell
Project Coordination, Text Design, and Electronic Page Makeup: Electronic Publishing
    Services Inc., NYC
Senior Design Manager: Nancy Danahy
Cover Designer: Kay Petronio
Cover Illustration: Copyright © Photodisc/Getty Images, Inc.
Manufacturing Buyer: Lucy Hebard
Printer and Binder: Courier Corporation
Cover Printer: Coral Graphic Services, Inc.

Library of Congress Cataloging-in-Publication Data

Rice, Jeff (Jeff R.)
    Writing about cool : hypertext and cultural studies in the computer classroom / Jeff Rice.
        p. cm.
    Includes bibliographical references and index.
    ISBN 0-321-10896-5 (pbk.)
        1. English language—Rhetoric—Computer-assisted instruction. 2. English
    language—Rhetoric—Study and teaching. 3. Report writing—Computer-assisted
    instruction. 4. Report writing—Study and teaching (Higher) 5. Cool (The English
    word) 6. Language and culture. 7. Hypertext systems. I. Title.

    PE1404.R513 2004
    808'.042'0285--dc22

                                                                    2003062366

Please visit our website at http://www.ablongman.com

ISBN 0-321-10896-5

1 2 3 4 5 6 7 8 9 10—CRS—06 05 04 03

CONTENTS

FOREWORD
Writing and Technology Series

The Writing and Technology Series offers introductory and supplementary textbooks for use in computer-and-writing and communication classes and in the humanities. This series focuses on instruction in writing hypertext, on development of electronic journals and multimedia projects, on assessment and evaluation of print versus electronic culture, on cultural studies and digital studies, the new technology and media, on MOOs as education sites, and on a variety of ever-growing educational concerns and challenges.

Writing About Cool is the third book in the series. Jeff Rice takes the word "cool" and develops it as a grand topos, or conceptual starting place, for thinking, reading, and writing in first-year and advanced writing classes. In calling on the cool, Rice is concerned with productively critiquing the various cultures we live in. As indicated by the subtitle of the book, *Hypertext and Cultural Studies in the Computer Classroom,* Rice is specifically concerned with introducing students not only to a writing of literacy (for print cultures) but also to a "writing" of electracy (electronic cultures). Hypertext here is not a limiting term, for multimedia with its hybrid genres are also included in the text and taught to students. In reading about how to apply the principles of writing cool/cool writing, students will learn how cool is one of those unique concepts as well as puncepts that has spanned many generations, cultures, races, social classes, and many genres and venues, and has many varied rhetorical strategies for expression and persuasion. Cool is for Rice, as it will be for students, a topos that can "bridge" us together in our many apparently disparate conversations about the past and what they can hold for us in building a more inclusive, humane future.

For a supplementary Web site for *Writing About Cool*, go to www.ablongman.com/rice/.

Victor J. Vitanza
Series Editor

PREFACE

This is a book about writing, technology, and cool. What does cool have to do with either writing or technology, you ask? Let me begin to explain by way of a personal example. I don't consider myself a "cool" person. In fact, as a writing instructor, my interest in computers and technology poses me more as a "geek" (or someone who wants to be a geek) than as someone who either is cool or is somehow connected to cool. And yet, when I surf the Web, a typical, comfortable, geek place, I constantly encounter this word. *Cool.* Site after site incorporates the word cool into its title: *Cool Archive, Cool Edit 2000, Cool Pet Stuff, Cool Uses for Cool.* Why, I ask, do so many people writing for the Web use the word *cool*? Why do Netscape, Yahoo, various e-mail bulletins and Web site updates all use this one word to describe their activities and services? Why are there a coolworks.com, a coolmath.com, a coolsavings.com, a coolgraphics.com, and so on, and not the same number of Web sites whose domains are devoted to other words? Does technology have anything to do with cool? Does the Web have anything to do with cool? What do all these sites have to do with me, the person who encounters them? What do these sites have to do with the technology I use for my own writing when I use the Web for work, research, and enjoyment? To make the question a broader one: does there exist a relationship between writing, technology, and cool?

These questions remind me of a recent IBM commercial for its Web service division. As the company's executives brainstorm an idea to make their product more attractive to consumers, one executive states that the organization needs to propose "something cool." The idea doesn't go down well with the boss, who moans that "Cool is why my son needs new shoes every month, why my daughter's hair is green. Cool costs me money." The executive who originally proposed the idea counters by stating, "This new online system will save us money, boss."

The boss replies, "Cool."

Like the IBM executive (and his boss), this book proposes *something cool.* And like IBM's interest in using technology for communicative purposes, this book finds various ways to connect technology and writing to a word that has had importance in our daily lives for almost a century. What companies like IBM understand, and what those of us in writing, cultural studies, and media studies classes need to understand, is cool's relevance to electronic culture and cool's relevance for learning how to write for electronic culture. As we write increasingly with new technologies like word processors, e-mail, MOOs, Weblogs, PowerPoint, and hypertext, and as we encounter cool in the electronic writings and images we read and see, we should consider the relationship between cool, writing, and technology at its various levels. If we want to understand how to communicate with technology, we first need to understand cool!

In this book, cool serves as both content (what this book is about) and as writing (a specific way to use technology to write). Consequently, this book challenges students and instructors to rethink traditional writing instruction. This may be the first time you (the student) or you (the instructor) have used a book with the word cool in its title for a college-level course (or any course, for that matter). You might ask, How can a textbook be about cool and at the same time teach cool as a way to write? Does cool, a word we use in everyday conversation with little attention to its meaning, have anything to do with the classroom, a place where we learn to analyze complex ideas, construct insightful responses, and write effectively? Can studying a subject matter (like cool) teach us specific ways to write? This book responds affirmatively: cool's presence and role in contemporary culture proves its relevance.

For instructors and students who use this book, I ask that you approach its thematic content, writing examples, and discussion and assignment prompts as a learning experience. Bring with you what you already know about cool, whether positive or negative, and treat this book as a place to use writing as a tool for learning more about something that we think we already know. Only when we rethink and explore familiar terms and ideas do we truly allow ourselves to learn. In that sense, this book, like the executives in the IBM commercial, *proposes something cool.*

Acknowledgments

Many people have helped shape this book. A significant debt is owed to the students who studied in the Writing About Cool courses I taught at the University of Florida. Without their insight and observations, much of this book's content would never have developed. I strongly thank Victor Vitanza for supporting this project with enthusiasm and encouragement. Without his support, I could never have written this text. I am in debt to Victor's influence and encouragement. At Allyn & Bacon/Longman, I extend gratitude to Joe Opiela for taking on this project and supporting my efforts as well as to Julie Hallett for answering all of my questions. I must acknowledge the friends in Gainesville, Detroit, and online with whom I've shared the ideas and assignments in this text, and who have often offered helpful comments and critique for their improvement and efficacy in teaching cool. I also thank the University of Detroit Mercy for encouraging me to bring my "cool" ideas to my current position as Director of Writing. In addition, I am grateful to Locke Carter, Texas Tech University; Scott Douglass, Chattanooga State Technical Community College; Dene Grigar, Texas Woman's University; Rich Rice, Texas Tech University; David Rogers, Valencia Community

College Osceola Campus; Peter Sands, University of Wisconsin-Milwaukee; and Janice Walker, Georgia Southern University, who each offered helpful suggestions on early versions of this book. I also thank Broward County Community College, Everything2.com, Clothestime, The Billboard Liberation Front, Yahoo!, and Netscape for permission to use images.

And, of course, I thank Sarika, who first pushed me to do this book and whose words of wisdom, phrased in her repetitive admonishment, "You're gonna get it," inspire a great deal of my writing and much of my life.

Jeff Rice
University of Detroit Mercy
riceje@udmercy.edu

Introduction:
What This Textbook Will Do

C ool is a way to write, a subject to write about, and an overall attitude that most of us can identify in some way, shape, or form. Beginning with this definition, *Writing About Cool* is an undergraduate composition/media studies textbook that uses all of these meanings in order to teach rhetorical approaches to writing for the World Wide Web. In particular, this textbook chooses the popular conception of cool as a means to understand both the cultural dimensions of electronic writing as well as the rhetorical strategies implicit in such writing.

The reason for associating cool with both technology and writing partly comes from the significant number of books published in the last few years that address these topics separately. These include: Marlene Kim Connor's *What is Cool? Understanding Black Manhood in America* (1995), Marcel Danesi's *Cool: The Signs and Meanings of Adolescence* (1994), Janet Mancini Billson and Richard Majors' *Cool Pose: The Dilemmas of Black Manhood in America* (1992), Gill Valentine and Tracey Skelton's *Cool Places: Geographies of Youth Cultures* (1998), Dick Pountain and David Robbins' *Cool Rules: Anatomy of An Attitude* (2000), and Lewis McAdams' *Birth of Cool* (2001). In the digital realm, Web design books have discovered in the word cool an appropriate marker for their work. Raul Razek's *Internet Cool Guide 2001* (2001), Dave Taylor's *Creating Cool HTML 4 Web Pages* (2000), and Paul M. Summitt and Mary J. Summitt's *Creating Cool Interactive Web Sites* (1996) are a few examples. The combination of cultural and electronic interest in cool suggests that both usages relate to one another, even if none of these books makes that suggestion explicit. This book attempts to explain the relationship between cool and technology by emphasizing the activity that bonds these two areas: writing. In order to do so, this book teaches cool as not just a subject to study, but as a new form of electronic writing as well.

Drawing upon cultural studies, media, literature, and the Web, cool writing answers the need for practical, pedagogical approaches to teaching and learning about electronic writing. Each chapter of this book details a media approach to cool and asks how particular media forms can serve as rhetorical models for a type of electronic writing called cool. The book's purpose, therefore, is to offer both analysis and a model as means towards writing about cool and towards cool writing. The thematic approach the book takes allows students to explore the complex meanings popular cultural vocabulary carries. It also demonstrates an approach that can be applied to other terms as well.

Education

This book recognizes the relationship between popular culture and education, focusing on how cool informs the way we learn. A May 2001 advertisement for Broward Community College in Fort Lauderdale, Florida, illustrates this notion nicely (see below).

Broward Community College taps into a common understanding of cool in order to market its educational programs to young people in southern Florida. The advertisement, in fact, demonstrates a good rhetorical usage of cool. When we come across an advertisement like this one, we need to ask why the school adapts cool as a way to sell its image. Why doesn't Broward Community College market itself by claiming, "Great School, Great Credits" or "Amazing School, Amazing Credits"? Cool must have been considered a more powerful, rhetorical option by the school's public relations department. Using cool to market educa-

**Broward Community College suggests
its education is "cool."**
Source: Used with permission of Broward Community College.

tion, Broward Community College most likely hopes to attract young students who might enroll elsewhere. Supposedly, prospective students will see the school as cool, as a worthwhile investment because it matches teenage lifestyle. Would you go to a school that advertised itself as cool?

As we'll see in this book, words like cool carry various meanings that provoke immediate responses. For instance, cool is often associated with the idea of rebellion or transgression. When a school posits its courses as cool, it suggests that its style of education rebels against traditional methods of teaching. Broward County Community College embraces cool so that students will believe that an education at this school will differ significantly from the negative learning experiences most students feel they've encountered. This ad, then, introduces us to one way cool functions as a form of writing; it appeals to youthful attitudes. Other forms of cool writing exist as well, and we'll learn about them as this book progresses.

This textbook begins with Broward Community College's usage of cool to create an urban, hip image by suggesting a connection between cool and learning. The moment higher education looks to cool as a means to increasing attendance, we need to rethink the role of cool, in general for education, and in particular for writing. We need to ask how popular culture terms like cool may serve us in unexpected ways. What kinds of meanings do everyday words contain, and how might these words become pedagogical at some point in their usage? In other words, this textbook makes a bold move. It asks you to think of language, and in particular one word, in a way you most likely have not done. It asks you to consider how a word like cool can teach us a great deal about writing.

What Kind of Writing Does This Book Teach?

While there are many ways to write electronically, *Writing About Cool* teaches hypertextual approaches to writing as they are informed by cultural studies. Before we explore cool as a topic for this book, we should first explore the other terms present in the book's title: hypertext and cultural studies. What do we mean by hypertext? Hypertext is the type of writing we encounter on the World Wide Web or in stand-alone computer systems like Storyspace and Hypercard. At its basic level, hypertext operates by nonlinear, associative linking. Written in HTML (hypertext markup language), hypertext's links and ability to absorb other computer languages (like JavaScript or DHTML) open up new possibilities for writers that print can't handle. In hypertext, ideas and images can interlink to create radically different perspectives, to build large databanks of interlinked information, or to store information for later retrieval. Originally theorized by Ted Nelson in the early 1960s, hypertext gained popularity when Tim Berners-Lee used it to invent the World Wide Web in the early 1990s.

When you surf the Web, the pages you read are connected by hypertext. When you click on a link, you are reading hypertext. The newspapers, fan sites, sports sites, and weather reports you read online are all written in hypertext. You may have even been asked to read such sites for past classes or to use online news-papers and journals for research in other classes. But have you ever been asked to write in hypertext? Throughout this book, we'll explore various approaches to hypertextual writing.

Our second question asks, what is cultural studies? Cultural studies is an area of inquiry that instructs readers and writers how to ask important questions about culture and the various assumptions we make regarding culture. For instance, we often maintain beliefs based on where we come from or how we define ourselves. What are our cultural backgrounds? Are we:

White descendants of European or Middle Eastern background
African-American
Hispanic
Native American
Asian-American
Male
Female
Heterosexual
Homosexual
Rich
Poor
Liberal
Conservative

Do we come from the suburbs, the country, or the city? Were we raised by two parents or one? What religion do we belong to? What kind of schools have we attended? Where have we worked? What kind of books, magazines, or news-papers do we read? What TV shows or films do we watch? What kind of music do we listen to? Cultural studies asks us to think about all of these questions whenever we read or write. It does so because all of these areas influence and shape the ideas we create. Cultural studies asks us to be aware of where our and others' ideas come from, to question the biases and assumptions we use to create such ideas, and to work towards a general understanding of each others' viewpoints. When we read and write from a cultural studies viewpoint, we study the places we work, politics, the language we use, the places we learn, and quite often, popular culture. We do so in order to ask questions. By asking these ques-tions, we gain deeper understandings of what we say and why we say it.

If we are to associate one action with cultural studies it might be, there-fore, *to question*.

For example, often cultural studies will examine how popular culture influ-ences the way we think. We might study shows like *Big Brother*, *The Real World*, *Joe Millionaire*, or *Survivor* and ask if and how these shows represent "reality." When conflict arises in these shows, is it natural or programmed? How does the editing of the show affect how we perceive the shows' story lines? Does the edit-ing create a story line different from what the participants may have experienced? Are the people who appear in these shows typical of "everyday people," or are they struggling actors looking for a big break, and thus "acting" emotional and distraught at times in order to highlight their skills?

Cultural studies also shows us ways to respond to questions of ideology and power, often by prompting us to examine cultural representations and ideas we normally take for granted. How do media create, for example, ideological impressions on readers and viewers? What is the power of representation? How do media representations affect our daily lives?

Continuing with our reality TV example, we might ask if these shows promote a specific ideology by capturing "real life" moments and displaying them to national viewers. Does *The Real World* challenge or reinforce "family values," for instance? What does the loaded expression "family values" mean when juxtaposed with a show like *The Real World*? Do the participants on *The Real World* practice an alternative kind of "family values," or are they, in fact, demonstrating the same kind of "family values" typically repeated by politicians or people with political agendas? And if we answer that the latter is true, how does that affect how we think of MTV in relationship to youth culture? If we find that *The Real World's* "family values" resemble the political right's "family values," then the "youth" angle of the show may be false. We might also consider how media representations may be used in subtle ways to promote specific ideological beliefs, often by masking those beliefs as alternatives to the status quo.

By asking these kinds of questions, cultural studies makes us think about how we respond to advertising, television programs, literature, music, and the Internet beyond immediate pleasure or dissatisfaction. Do these media affect us in other meaningful ways? Do minority groups respond to and create meanings in the same way that dominant groups do? Do both teenagers and adults always respond to music the same way? What is the influence of consumerism upon our daily lives? Do we shop at a particular store because of the images its advertisements have created for us? Or do we just go to get what we need? All of these questions belong to the rich tradition of cultural studies.

For the most part, textbooks influenced by cultural studies approach these questions from the position of analysis. To understand advertising's affect on culture, for example, such textbooks ask readers to decode the messages advertisers proliferate. One typical reading of this sort might claim that the Marlboro Man symbolizes the cowboy lifestyle. This reading then asks you to question Marlboro's association of its product with the cowboy lifestyle (if you smoke this brand of cigarettes, you'll be, in effect, a cowboy). This version of cultural studies asks students to become proficient readers and to write about their reading experiences. *Writing About Cool* begins from this valuable position, but it also asks student-readers to become media-writers. Media teach us new methods of persuasion and argumentation nonexistent or little practiced in print-based writing. Advertising, for example does specific things with texts and images that make it an important media form. How does advertising bring together distinct images? How does it utilize widely held beliefs? When you watch a Nike or Reebok commercial, how does the commercial mix images of athletes with the shoes they're wearing? Why does it do so? *How* does it do so?

In the tradition of cultural studies, *Writing About Cool* asks many questions like these, only it asks you to perform similarly in your own writing in order to:

1. Learn how meanings are constructed
2. Construct your own meanings

More generally, this book questions how we write about culture in a media-dominated culture, one which is quick to embrace the digital age and all of its applications: the Web, video, DVD, wireless communication, etc. Do the old ways of writing hold up, or must we append them and consider the way new media functions?

How This Book Works

Writing About Cool follows the cultural studies tradition by focusing on one popular culture form, cool. Cool represents an idea most of us are familiar with. Yet, we probably haven't asked how a concept like cool is socially, economically, or even racially constructed. By studying cool from a cultural studies perspective, we can carefully examine how a great deal of culture—and in particular, digital culture—is shaped by the notion of cool. Even more so, we can see how cool turns into a form of writing through these various approaches. In turn, we can create an electronic form of critique (that is, questioning) called cool. Unlike other applications of cultural studies in pedagogy, however, this textbook proposes that critique comes from the media itself; i.e., we can learn from the ways media form ideological positions to critique those very positions. In other words, we can learn a great deal from the ways cool is formed and spread throughout society.

Writing About Cool uses our cultural understandings of the concept of cool to fashion alternative approaches to writing. *Writing About Cool* suggests that we can learn from various meanings of cool (all of which will be explored in this book) in order to create hypertextual writings. Why should we want to write in hypertext? Currently, we receive ever-increasing amounts of information from the Web: stock reports, news, entertainment, etc. But in order to contribute to this writing environment, we also need to know how to write for it, not just how to read it.

Writing hypertext means not just learning its technical demands, like how to make a hyperlink or how to put an image on a page, but how to write rhetorically in hypertext. Often we learn rhetorical strategies for print ranging from the inclusion of stylistic tropes and figures to the recognition of one's perceived audience and adaptation of one's writing to that specific audience. Typically, a writing class might ask you to locate topic sentences in readings and then form them in your own writing. Or a class might demonstrate how to develop supporting sentences for your topic sentence, or even how to write a conclusion to your work. Eventually, you may also be asked to produce several drafts of an assignment and to comment on various changes you've made to each draft.

These are important steps towards learning to write, whether one writes for electronic or print media. Because numerous textbooks already address these points, however, *Writing About Cool* does not treat them in detail. Because *Writing About Cool* focuses on electronic writing, it emphasizes new challenges to being rhetorically persuasive and effective.

In other words, what if you don't want to just write *about* digital culture, but you want to *write* digitally?

Go to the Web site for the magazine *21C*: http://www.21cmagazine.com/.

Then visit the Web site for the White House: http://www.whitehouse.gov/.

Then take a look at the Web site for the University of Florida's Networked Writing Environment: http://www.nwe.ufl.edu/writing/.

Each site is different, yet each site offers an example of digital writing. Instead of analyzing what these sites say (in other words, what they mean), we'll try to understand how sites like these organize and present information rhetorically. Throughout this book, we'll study how various media forms (like Web sites) organize information, and then we'll attempt our own hypertextual writing at the end of each chapter.

This book, however, will not teach you how to make a Web page. Excellent online and textbook documentation has already been developed for a wide audience, from the novice to the expert, for that purpose. We assume that you already have or are receiving instruction in HTML. If you need further help with HTML, the Web site accompanying this book will provide you with tips and resources for your work.

What this textbook offers are approaches for combining cultural studies and writing hypertext. Other than merely uploading standard papers to the Web or analyzing whether particular Web sites are accurate sources of information or not, are there ways to be effective as hypertext writers? Are there new writing approaches we need to learn? What is different in hypertext than in print? What is the same? How do writers in hypertext organize information? How do they display their ideas in order to be persuasive? *Writing About Cool* asks these questions as it develops alternative strategies regarding the topic of cool. In other words, we will use each definition of cool as a model for writing in hypertext.

In each chapter you will read about various ways cool is expressed. Our reason for explaining these meanings of cool is that we want you to consider its multitude of applications and how those very applications can be used as models for hypertextual writings. We encourage you to go to the Web sites we discuss and see firsthand how these sites use cool in terms of content and form. We also encourage you to expand your understandings of cool by viewing the recommended films and by reading the additional selections we provide at the end of each chapter. These recommendations are meant to further help you understand cool's potential for writing.

Because cool is such a widely used term, we ask that you bring your prior knowledge of cool with you as you read through this book. In fact, one of the main reasons cool is the topic of this book is because most of us already have developed some kind of understanding of the term. Most likely we use the word to express satisfaction with an event's results, someone's look or attitude, or what we feel about a particular item. "That's cool" remains one of our most widely used expressions. Therefore, we want to begin with what you already think about when you hear the word cool. We also ask, however, that you consider the other definitions we will discuss. Throughout this textbook, we'll be encountering ideas and definitions of cool you have probably never heard before. In turn, we will see that cool means a number of things. Taken together, these definitions will teach us a great deal about writing, for all of these definitions will form various ways to engage with cool writing.

Chapter

The Cool Media

The word cool carries many meanings. Most of us use the term daily in conversation or at least encounter it regularly in various media. Television shows, movies, popular songs, magazines, newspapers, and Web sites all employ the term in one way or another at any given moment. Sometimes cool appears as "kewl." Sometimes it even shows up as "kool." You're probably familiar with expressions like "real cool cucumber," "cool out," "be cool," or "cool, man."

We normally think of cool as a word that describes someone who is "in," "popular," or "hip." For hip-hop pioneer and graffiti artist Fab Five Freddy, cool has come to mean "a form of approval" picked up by urban youth to convey their feelings about what they like. When we say "that's cool" or, as hip-hop group Digable Planets states, "It's cool like that," we are using cool in the manner Fab Five Freddy suggests; we are indicating an overall feeling that something (or someone) is worthwhile. Writer Michael Jarrett, on the other hand, defines cool as either prophetic cool—"characterized by barely harnessed rage"—or philosophical cool—"the existential void lurking behind a persona." What Jarrett refers to are the ways cool has been used to describe particular personality types. In popular culture, we can identify these two definitions with a variety of personalities. James Dean might typify the prophetic version of cool, the angry young man rebelling against his parents or society in general. Johnny Depp or Kurt Cobain could be classified as philosophical cool, the brooding figure who is attractive because of aloofness and distance from the rest of us.

> Make a list of all the definitions of cool you can think of. Then make a list of all the expressions you've heard that use the word cool.

When we think of the word cool, we often imagine a rebel, an outcast, or a teenager who feels alienated. In the 1950s and 1960s, the image of James Dean or Marlon Brando wearing a plain white t-shirt or dressed in a leather jacket—a look of discontent on their faces—captured our imaginations in this regard. In fact, even someone who has never seen a James Dean or Marlon Brando film will usually recognize these images. In particular, we recognize the image because of the ubiquitous posters, postcards, photographs, and t-shirts that show Dean or Brando as a tough guy looking aloof and distant, wearing a white t-shirt and maybe standing next to a motorcycle. Today, such attitudes and images are expressed by popular cultural personalities like Snoop Dogg or Jay-Z, hip-hop performers who have appropriated much of the 1950s look in order to express angst and frustration through their appearance as well as their music.

Cool teenagers are often those who feel constrained by their families, their schools, their jobs, or their relationships and seek new meanings in life that oppose the system they've long been a part of. The way they demonstrate this opposition earns the moniker cool. If a singer like Madonna is cool, we think so because of the way she makes her own stand in the world, and the way she rebels against societal expectations of a woman's behavior by adapting personas deemed excessive or outlandish. If we think rap singer Tupac Shakur is cool, it is because he has embraced an outlaw persona, the gangster, a role outside of mainstream society. Gangsters live on the edge. They confront authority figures. They face death daily.

Each of these ideas represents a popular perception of cool:

- Independence: The individual does what she/he wants to do without regard for society's rules and regulations.
- Rebelliousness: Part of being independent includes rebelling against the rules society has created. Cool people interpret these rules as restrictive and conformist. Thus, there exists a need to rebel and demonstrate independence.

All in all, cool is a word most often associated with behavior or personality traits. To say that someone is cool normally indicates that we think highly of that person. We admire these cool traits. We do so, however, not so much out of respect but out of mystique. In other words, something about that individual creates a sense of mystery, of otherness, of excitement and intrigue. There is something about a cool person that we want to see in ourselves, but often are too timid to embrace. If we can't be cool, at least we can appreciate it and marvel over it in others. Cool personas, then, involve image. The way we interpret cool people involves a contrast between how we see ourselves and how we see others. When we recognize an exceptional difference in another person's image, we deem that individual cool.

On May 29, 2001, *USA Today* published a list of responses from its survey, "Pop Culture: What's Cool?" Respondents noted items as diverse as "jeans with the top cut off," "Steve McQueen," "*Sex and the City*," "toys from the '80s," and "hot rods." The April 11, 2002, issue of *Rolling Stone* was subtitled "The Cool Issue." It included elaborate lists of cool people, thoughts, items, and events.

- Why do you think these publications are interested in listing and surveying feelings about what or who is cool?

- Do they search for consensus?

- Do they want to show how diverse cool is to different audiences?

- Which of the items in the *USA Today* list do you agree with?

- What might your own list of cool items look like?

Cool on the Internet

On the Internet, the association of "cool" with rebellion and mystique has been adopted by a significant number of Web sites and Web services. The preponderance of Web sites embracing cool as a descriptive term of Web site content or design deserves a closer look. Typing the word cool into any number of search engines like Google (http://www.google.com), Yahoo (http://www.yahoo.com), or Go2net (http://www.go2net.com) brings up thousands of hits. Entering cool into the search engines of a variety of online merchants like booksellers Amazon (http://www.amazon.com) or Barnes and Noble (http://www.barnesandnoble.com) likewise produces an extraordinary response. While not all the resulting listings relate to the term we commonly know as cool, a majority, in some form, tap into the word's popular connotation of "hip," "good," "in," or some other form of approval.

Take note of these distinct sites that incorporate the word cool into their titles:

- Cool Bank (http://www.coolbank.com)
- Cool Nurse (http://www.coolnurse.com)
- Cool Grrrls (http://www.coolgrrrls.com)
- Cool Jobs (http://www.cooljobs.com)

How differently does each site apply the word cool? How are the sites similar? Why has cool metamorphosed into a popular word, not only in daily conversation, but on the Internet as well? Does using this specific word help persuade Web surfers to visit these sites? Why?

In the next chapter, we'll examine in more detail various sites utilizing cool for different reasons. For now, think of how these sites establish (or attempt to establish) an electronic method of expression based on the word cool. How does the word function in order to attract an audience and get its attention?

The purpose of this textbook is to begin to understand how a personality trait like cool has become a form of expression on the Internet and in electronic culture in general. Instead of offering a history of cool and the Web, however, we'll examine a variety of media forms, including Internet sites, to see how cool is used. Our purpose is not merely to study cool as a subject like math, biology, or history. Rather, we want to learn how cool has been transformed from a personality trait into an electronic writing strategy so that we can participate in such writing as well.

Throughout this textbook, we'll examine various media forms including the World Wide Web, advertising, literature, and music. Each form will teach us an approach to cool as electronic writing. We won't necessarily be analyzing each form's content—though we will do so periodically for specific reasons—but we will consider how media is constructed in relationship to cool. The continuing question we will ask is: What is the rhetoric of cool media? We don't necessarily want to settle on one answer, but rather on a number of possibilities.

Rhetoric means the way people express themselves, form arguments, explain situations, and attempt to get an idea across to an audience. Rhetoric includes the various tools we use (in writing and in speaking) to create such expression. To be rhetorically effective, we may appeal to an audience's emotions or desires. We may employ metaphors or similes. We might even construct complex associations that trigger a desired reaction.

But is there such a thing as a rhetoric to cool writing beyond thinking about personality or individual characteristics? Saying that there exists a rhetoric to cool writing indicates specific writing strategies conducive to the concept of cool. The word's ubiquitous nature in everyday life suggests such a rhetoric; in other words, its repetitive usage indicates it's being used for specific rhetorical strategies. Can one write cool? How does cool guide our writing in the twenty-first century? These questions will be addressed throughout this book. In the next chapter, we'll begin with the Web.

Class Discussion

1. Make a list of various toys, games, events, people, places, songs, TV shows, and other items you consider cool. As a class, compare your lists. Note the overlaps. Note the discrepancies. Can you agree on one list?
2. Why are there so many sites with the word "cool" in their domain? Why not some other word? What other words might serve the same purpose as cool does?
3. What other terms create a "rhetoric"? Is cool the only one?

Exercises: A Museum of Cool Sites

1. Construct a museum of cool Internet sites. By this, we don't mean find sites you consider to exemplify "cool," but rather construct an inventory of as many sites that you can find using cool in their title, content, or lists.

   Put your findings together on a Web site so that they create a virtual museum, an exhibition of cool on the Internet.
2. Construct a similar site for "cool" people. In constructing this site, decide first the characteristics of "cool" you will use to make the site. Make a list of such characteristics. Then use these traits to guide your decisions.

   How will you organize your museum? By body posture? Clothing? Attitude?

   Could images alone create a definition of the cool person? Do you need to include commentary? What kind?

Chapter

2

Surfing the Internet for Cool

Our first step toward understanding how to write cool is to examine cool's place on the Internet, since the Internet is today one of the most popular places for displaying hypertextual writing. In this chapter, we'll look at the fascination with cool among several popular Web sites. By examining each site's interest in cool, we'll see the relationship the Internet maintains with cool by way of both electronic writing and consumer culture. The rhetorical moves various Internet sites make can give us new ideas regarding how to use this word for our own writing. By the end of the chapter, our focus will shift as we examine Web sites that not only use cool as a word to draw in readers, but that actually produce writing for the Web called cool.

Current excitement over the Internet stems from the 1993 development of the Web browser Mosaic, the first browser capable of displaying graphics. Prior to Mosaic, Web sites were limited to text, which was possibly one reason for its minimal usage (at least in comparison with the amount of surfing done today). The text-based Web attracted only a small number of viewers and creators of sites. Its purpose was mostly to share information among scientists and academics, as well as to provide a communal meeting ground for electronically savvy computer users who could share knowledge and form social groups. After the development and distribution of Mosaic, and shortly thereafter Netscape 2.0, this small group of Web users sparked the Internet revolution. Their usage of the Web to distribute not only scientific information, but also personal and entertainment-based content, attracted a quickly growing audience.

Such users congregated on places like TheWell.com, a one-time haven for those interested in both technology and 1960s counterculture attitudes. The Well (Whole Earth 'Lectronic Link) used a BBS (bulletin board system) to create a virtual community. Members logged on and talked with one another through the electronic bulletin board, a text-based message system where notes are posted for all to see and respond to. Although not all Well members were leftover hippies of the 1960s, many of the participants had grown up in that time period. They saw the emerging Internet as a place for free speech and an open sharing of information, in the absence of racism, sexism, and class distinctions. For these users, the Web mirrored the antiauthority attitudes of the sixties. Some Well members, like former Grateful Dead song writer and Electronic Frontier Foundation founder John Perry Barlow, voiced strong opinions regarding the future of the Internet, proposing a democratic utopia reminiscent of the 1960s' Flower Power movement or 1967's Summer of Love. As children of the sixties, they also brought with them a word they had grown up using regularly as part of the antiestablishment movement: cool. We might suggest that through early online groups like The Well, cool moved to the Internet where it eventually became a term indicative of interesting and unique sites one should visit on the Web.

- How important is it that early users of the Internet had participated in the countercultural attitudes of the 1960s? Do you think this leftover feeling of rebellion might have contributed to the dominance of the word cool on the Internet today? In other words, do terms popular with one generation (as cool was to the young people of the 1960s) play important roles later on in other areas of expression (like the Internet)? We might ask, then, how the rhetoric (the various meanings) surrounding a popular term can be used in other areas at a later date.
- How do "countercultural" groups (and we're leaving this term largely undefined) use the word cool today? Does cool still mean rebellion? Or does it mean other things as well?

Cool Sites

One of the earliest Web sites to use the word cool was Netscape, a Web portal that provides a search engine for Web surfing as well as extensive preconstructed listings of Web sites. Search engines give users the ability to navigate the rich resources the Internet offers. Typically, results are returned to the user in long listings of sites. Netscape adapted the rhetoric surrounding cool (good, worthwhile) in order to deem its listings of worthwhile sites on the Internet to visit as cool sites. Netscape used to justify its site listings by stating:

> Someday we'll all agree on what's cool on the Net. In the meantime, the Netscape cool team will continue to bring you a list of select sites that catch our eyes, make us laugh, help us work, quench our thirst…you get the idea.

Currently, Netscape has updated this policy as follows:

> What Makes Us the Arbiters of Cool?
> It takes a willingness on our part to apply well-honed skills of judgment, together with a certain savoir faire. Of course, no one can claim to be the definitive source of cool even though we're trying. Meanwhile, we refuse to hoard cool URLs solely for our own enjoyment.

We can learn something about cool, Web surfing, and the Internet from the Netscape example. Netscape uses the word cool not only for site listings but also as a way to connect visitors to its Web site with other sites, often sites Netscape maintains business partnerships with. In this way, Netscape is using the word cool rhetorically. The portal's purpose is to figure out how this word will persuade readers to use its services or use the services Netscape has established with other companies

For example, when Netscape asks its readers "How Cool Are You?" (originally located at http://home.netscape.com/netcenter/cool.html, but now only viewable through its cached file on Google: http://www.google.com/search? q=cache:iMF4031R8AE:home.netscape.com/netcenter/2000/sept/0922_cool.htm l%3Fcp%3Dlastweekn+%22How+Cool+are+You%3F%22+%2B+Netscape&hl=en), it answers its own question with links to outlets on the World Wide Web that sell electronic goods like MP3 players, DVDs, and compact discs. At times, the Web portal goes as far as to list brand names (CNN, TV Guide, Moviefone) as examples of cool, all in the interest of helping these companies market their products to large audiences.

The rhetorical lesson here is that Netscape provides a good example of how the word cool has been commercialized. By using a word that is familiar to most of its readers, and by repeating a word that is popular in everyday conversation, Netscape is able to place promotional activities in the foreground without the appearance of doing so. We can generalize two initial important points relevant to our own writing:

- Words that we use daily without careful consideration can be manipulated for ulterior motives, in this case, monetary gain. But the possibilities can be generalized to other results.
- We can use common words (like cool) in order to be persuasive. Instead of selling goods and services, we can use such words as tools to get a readership to believe a specific point or cause we are espousing.

> Why do you think Netscape equates brand names with the word cool? What might be the consequences of this action? We'll talk about brand names more shortly, so keep this in mind for now.

The Netscape example appears elsewhere on the Web. Yahoo, a Web portal like Netscape, also provides site listings under the name cool. Yahoo Cool Links (http://dir.yahoo.com/entertainment/cool_links/index.html) and its subdirectory, Cool Yahoo! Categories (http://dir.yahoo.com/Entertainment/cool_links/ cool_yahoo_categories/) offer readers what it considers the "best of the Web." Divided up into several areas, Yahoo's Cool Categories section includes such offerings as Beat Generation, Music that Sucks, Reality Television, and Web Art. Yahoo's connection between cool and salesmanship may not always be as apparent as Netscape's, but clicking through some of Yahoo's categories unveils the site's financial interests. One category, Music that Sucks, for example, contains a link to Yahoo's Shopping: Music guide, a service the site offers for selling compact discs. By clicking on Music that Sucks, viewers may believe they are being transported to independent Web sites hosting musical opinions. In fact, the site connected by the link is merely another part of Yahoo's holdings.

When encountering these types of applications of cool, we need to question the host site's rhetorical choice of links. To which sites do they connect? Why? Are we really being transported to a new site, or are we still within the site where we started? What does it mean to see sites like Yahoo use cool to create economic relationships with other services?

Such questions immediately alter the way we read and write for the Web. How many times do you visit Web portals like Netscape or Yahoo and follow links without asking why they lead to certain sites rather than others? Do you trust Web portals to deliver content and not advertising? What assumptions do you make about sites like Yahoo and Netscape when you first visit them? We need to keep these questions in mind as we examine these sites' usage of cool for marketing purposes.

Similar to Yahoo, Cool Zones (http://cool.infi.net/zones.html) promises to be "the place to find the coolest of the cool with a minimum of effort." Like Yahoo and Netscape, it lists out of the ordinary or supposedly interesting sites worth visiting. Cool Zones belongs to a long list of Web sites and e-mail services that promote the "cool site of the day." As a way to encourage Web surfing, "cool sites of the day" supposedly deserve extra attention for some special service or content. And like various sites, Cool Zones offers "special offers and shopping deals" through prearranged financial relationships with various retail outlets like Staples, Barnes & Noble, and Gap. Most evident at Cool Zones' main page (http://cool.infi.net/home.html), many of these "cool sites of the day" are, in fact, based on such arrangements. On Cool Zones, what classifies as a "cool deal" is a reciprocal arrangement between Cool Zones and any given retail outlet.

> At what point do we differentiate between brand names and information content? Is there a difference? Does a brand name ever stand for the content itself? For example, how does the name Nike always state something specific about the company's image?

What these sites tell us is that the attitudes we associate with a word like cool (rebellion, uniqueness, popularity) are subject to being used rhetorically for consumer purposes. Why label a sale a "cool deal" and not a "great deal," a "fantastic deal," or a "wonderful deal"? The reason is that the word cool maintains a special place in our cultural vocabulary. These sites have developed a rhetorical application of cool, one that draws upon the word's cultural connotations in order to attract an audience. Using cool can increase sales if it is marketed at an appropriate audience, which usually means teenagers.

For instance, if you think of why Yahoo labels its music link "Music that Sucks," you might consider that words like "suck" carry specific relevance for youth culture. Teenagers might feel more inclined to click on a link titled "Music that Sucks" rather than a link that merely states "Music." But doesn't "suck" mean something bad? Yes. Similar to the "cool deals" example, however, using a word with teenage meaning (like suck) will attract a young audience more than words like "bad," "not good," or "awful." Such moves will be the subject of our next section: the relationship between youth culture and the Web. For now, we can see that the mere mention of a loaded word like cool or suck can persuade viewers to read on, a point you should consider when you write for the Web and begin to think about how to construct hypertext links.

Some words have powerful meanings because of cultural associations we've aligned with them. Cool is one such word. What are some others?

If you were to use the word "suck" in an academic paper for one of your classes, what would be the instructor's likely reaction? If you used the word with your friends, what might be their reaction?

We need to always be aware of who we are writing for (or communicating with) when we choose words.

Indeed, the economic relationships sites like Netscape, Yahoo, and Cool Zones build are geared, to a large extent, to developing ties with companies that cater to teenagers. While early users of the Web used cool as a reminder of the anti-authority idealism of their youth, current applications of cool are designed to appeal to teenagers with purchasing power. Those same teenagers relate the word to style and popularity. Together, Web sites bank on the chance that youth will buy goods within this category. We can trace the rhetorical meanings of cool as a series of shifts:

- Prior to the Internet—cool means rebellion, individuality, mystique.
- After the Internet—cool means an attractive tool for luring potential customers.

Hold on to these definitions as we examine other Web sites' usage of cool. Where do these definitions intersect? Where do they contradict one another?

Youth, Design, and Cool Web Sites

Often, sites that provide cool listings see cool as a marker of youth culture. By linking with a retailer such as Gap, for instance, Yahoo identifies a significant amount of its readership as young, and most likely as teenagers. Yahoo even maintains a separate site called Yahooligans! Cool! (http://www.yahooligans.com/docs/cool/) specifically aimed to a young, teenage audience. Yahooligans! Cool! presents itself as an educational site. Its listings aren't geared to teenagers searching for information on their favorite rock band, but rather to those who seek out further reading on topics like the universe, amusement parks, and world history. Yahooligans! Cool! restructures the word cool in order to say "learning can be fun."

Cool.com also appeals to a young audience in a similar, educational way, only its focus is directed more towards popular culture. Cool.com tells its readers, "You know what's cool. We'll show you what's hot." Cool.com appears to be geared to a teenage audience familiar with MTV's *Total Request Live* program, an audience eager for gossip on its favorite bands or TV actors. A great deal of Cool.com is devoted to such content. The site's Cool Wish Box features fashion tips, gaming advice, and band updates. Cool.com anchors the word cool to the Internet by providing yourname@cool.com free e-mail, identifying its members' online names with the word cool. In the advertising chapter, we'll see how important personal identification is in cool.

Go online and visit Cool 2B Real (http://www.cool-2b-real.com/). What specific youth-oriented audience is this site directed towards? How do you know? What images and text lead you to that conclusion?

Writing Cool

Project Cool, on the other hand, differs slightly from these previous examples in that it lists Web sites that grant "knowledge, guidance, and inspiration to Web designers and developers." In this way, Project Cool's version of cool listings turns the idea of cool back onto the Web itself, linking cool with hands-on electronic know-how. Project Cool marks a good place to think about how the word cool influences Web design. The other sites mentioned here find a correlation between the Internet and cool, but they do so at the level of marketing, selling their products to as large a potential client base as possible. Marketing teaches us how words are used to attract given audiences. Project Cool takes us in another direction; it allows us to think of how the word cool may have larger implications for writing on the Web, that is, for writing hypertext.

The Yahooligans! Cool! Web site.
Source: Reproduced with permission of Yahoo! Inc. © 2003 by Yahoo! Inc. YAHOO! and the YAHOO! logo are trademarks of Yahoo! Inc.

Hypertext is the form of writing we encounter when we surf the Web. Hypertext is constructed in HTML (hypertext markup language). HTML differs from the type of writing you may be used to doing when you use a word processing program like Word or WordPerfect; it requires writers to include special codes in their writing. When we create a document in a word processing program, these codes exist, but they are hidden from us. In HTML, these codes are called *tags*; they tell a browser (a graphic-reading interface like Netscape, Mozilla, or Microsoft's Explorer that allows users to view Web pages) how to format text, include images, make things on a Web page move, etc.

Project Cool takes the word cool and relates it to the idea of writing in HTML. Its Developer Zone includes an extensive library of tips on how to create Web pages appropriate for beginners as well as novices. The site implies that these tips are not only cool, but that those who apply the tips to their own work are cool as well. Project Cool, then, marks our first visit to an Internet site that defines cool as a particular form of writing, and, in particular, as hypertext writing.

Similar to Project Cool, the Web site Everything2.com connects the word cool to writing hypertext. Only instead of providing readers with lists of instructional Web sites, Everything2.com is a content-based Web site where users log in so that they can discuss various topics with one another. These conversations are interlinked extensively with one another through the site's complex system of interlinking. On a typical entry in Everything2.com, you may be reading one user's short essay on a topic, and in that essay each word may link to another related essay written by someone else. Everything2.com calls this interlinking *cooling*. Its users (who are called noders) *cool* topics by interlinking them with others throughout the site's membership base. Cool, therefore, functions as a verb and not just as a noun; it describes a way to write. In Chapter 14, we'll discuss Everything2.com's cool writing in more detail. In the meantime, a quick visit to Everything2.com reveals how noders discuss various issues related to popular culture such as popular fashions, music, eating, film, and television.

Most of these discussions take place in Everything2.com's Page of Cool and Cream of Cool sections. What makes this site interesting is how noders find ways to create connections between subjects we normally wouldn't consider related. Cooling means creating these connections; it means seeing areas that interest us as being interrelated. Instead of thinking of Japanese cuisine and punk music, for example, as separate areas of interest, noders try to cool these areas. They search out new connections that we previously hadn't considered.

Have you ever questioned why school subjects are separate? Why do you have one class for chemistry, one for English, one for history, and so forth? Each discipline has its own distinct area of specialization and study. But aren't there also moments when you notice connections between the various classes you take? Based on Everything2.com's definition, joining your classes together via various words or ideas would be called cooling.

After visiting Everything2.com, consider how this type of writing differs from a print-based explanation of a given topic. In other words, locate rhetorical differences. For instance, nodes on Everything2.com tend to be short and fragmented. Fragmented doesn't mean that entries are not written in complete sentences or in complete thoughts, but rather that they are brief. When you follow the various links between the fragmented entries, you find yourself reading complete ideas and arguments, even though they are often written by different people. In this way, noders collaborate with one another. Their entries create collages that, when read differently, can create alternative reading experiences with each click of the mouse. How else does this type of writing differ from the print-based assignments you are used to doing for your classes? Can you identify other rhetorical differences?

Everything2.com demonstrates how writing about cool on the Web can be more than a listing of sites to visit. Everything2.com also teaches us that cool itself can be thought of as writing. On Everything2.com, one doesn't write, one cools. We'll examine this Web site in more depth later in this book when we discuss hypertext as cool writing.

What does that mean, though, in the larger scope of things? How can writing be cool? Can you write cool? This brief survey of sites that use cool in a variety of ways, from listings to actual critical writing, is meant as a demonstration of how cool currently influences expression on the Web. Whether cool is used as a word meaning "places to visit" or as a key word for creating Web pages or even, as Everything2.com shows, an actual writing system, we see a connection between cool and electronic writing. In particular, Everything2.com

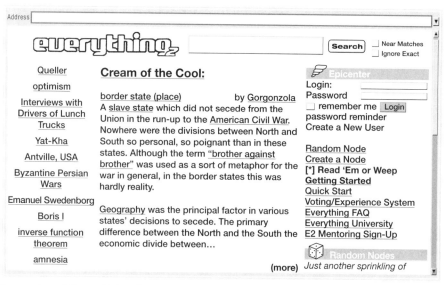

Example of Everything2.com's Cream of the Cool. Each underlined word is a link that "cools" the writer's ideas.
Source: Used with permission of Everything2.com.

demonstrates the movement of cool from marketing tool to writing system. All of these examples, therefore, can be generalized to our own writing and teach us new ways of expression.

Further Reading

Negroponte, Nicholas. *Being Digital*. New York: Vintage, 1995.
Rheingold, Howard. *The Virtual Community: Homesteading on the Electronic Frontier*. New York: HarperPerennial, 1994. Online version available at: http://www.rheingold.com/vc/book/.

Films to Watch

The Blackboard Jungle. Dir. Richard Brooks. Perf. Sidney Poitier. MGM, 1955. This film offers a portrayal of 1950s youth attitudes in the public school system, showing teenagers rebelling against the school's authority system. It marks an important reminder of where Web sites like Yahoo get their ideas from.
The Wild One. Dir. László Benedek. Perf. Marlon Brando. Columbia Pictures, 1954. Another good example of teenage attitudes regarding rebellion.

Web Site

Visit this book's Web site for further examples of cool writing similar to the online examples discussed in this chapter.

Class Discussion

1. What are your first impressions of the word cool? How did our look at the application of cool on the World Wide Web enforce or alter that perception? How do the Web sites discussed here support our previous understanding of cool?
2. Why is the Web entrenched in consumerism? Does it have to be this way? Do Web portals have to sell goods? How do you feel about the subtle ways cool is used to sell products? Is there something wrong with using cool to sell commercial goods? Or is it an acceptable practice? Why or why not?
3. What other words on the Web are used to sell products the way cool is used?
4. Visit the sites mentioned in this chapter. How different are their approaches to cool? Why does cool fit with each site's overall strategy? Could another word have worked as well? Why or why not?

Exercises: The Everything2.com Assignment

1. Use the cool Web site listing phenomenon as a rhetorical model for further writing. These sites teach us that there exists on the Web a deep interest in serving the surfing community with recommendations of places to visit. Instead of listing "cool" sites, pick another topic (not cool) and create your

own list in hypertext. Research the Web for sites that fit that topic. For example, instead of creating a listing of cool Web sites, you could create listings of sports sites, fashion sites, or food sites. Each item in your list should link to their respective sites.

Think about your site in terms of classification. How do Netscape and Yahoo classify what is cool? Are there subheadings? Unique sections? Out of the ordinary sections? How will you classify your topic? Yahooligans! Cool! alters the word cool in order to create its list. Does your topic allow for similar manipulations?

2. Then use Everything2.com as a model to create a new project. Rather than simply list sites as you have done already, cool your findings (using the Everything2.com definition of cool) and observations on your findings. Use hypertext links to create associations between various areas you have discovered. What kind of effect will your work have on readers when you join unlike items together through the hyperlink? What kind of effects can you create by doing so?

What will you link to? What do the writers of Everything2.com link to? Are there expanded definitions? Excerpts from previously published material (interviews, song lyrics, newspaper stories)?

Nodes on Everything2.com tend to be fragmented and brief. By reading through the various fragments, one gets a clear understanding of the topic discussed. The focus of your writing, then, should be to create short, fragmented thoughts that when linked together create one idea.

You might benefit by first mapping out your ideas on paper. Do a storyboard—a visualization of what you intend to do that looks like a series of comic strips. Look at the language you are using, the ideas you are creating. Where do they connect?

3. As a class, cool all of the class members' work into one giant Page of Cool. Allow similar ideas and words to interlink. What is the overall effect of such a piece of writing? When placed in juxtaposition with one another, how have your ideas transformed? As you connect each class member's work to another's, what are the reasons for doing so? Does each individual work change as it links up to other works simultaneously?

4. An alternative exercise would be to do the same thing for the classes you take. Do an inventory of all of the readings and discussion you are having in each class this semester. Look for common words, ideas, concepts, and terms that reappear in each class. It doesn't matter, for example, if the word means the same thing in English as it does in physics. Make a list of these patterns you have discovered.

Write a hypertextual narrative about your classes, and cool your narrative with hyperlinks the way Everything2.com users do. The patterns you have found will allow you to create intricate connections between your areas of study.

Chapter

3

Advertising

The Cool Ad

In this chapter, we'll take a close look at the relationship between advertising and cool. Following our work in Chapter 2, we'll consider how cool serves advertising's financial needs by providing an attractive forum for youth culture. In addition, we'll explore how certain groups use cool in order to resist the lures of advertising. These groups will grant us additional models for our own hypertextual writing.

Advertising has typically followed the development of new media forms. When we speak of media, we mean sources of information and entertainment. Movies, magazines, newspapers, books, television, radio, and now the Internet are all examples of media. Advertising serves other media by allowing producers of content to be financially compensated for their work. Television, for example, makes money by inserting commercials between broadcasts. Radio does the same. And even film performs similarly. Think of the advertisements that precede the featured attraction.

The Internet, then, performs no differently than previous media forms. On the Internet, advertising's interest in cool resembles what we see on Web sites like Netscape or Yahoo. Advertisers have been quick to understand that terms familiar to youth culture can be *appropriated* and redone in order to serve their own economic interests.

Appropriation means taking an idea, object, or style from its original context and redoing it in a manner different from its original purpose. Thomas Frank, a critic of popular culture, writes in his book *The Conquest of Cool: Business Culture, Counterculture, and the Rise of Hip Consumerism* that the attitude we commonly associate with cool has become a staple for advertisers' marketing campaigns, which appropriate cool for commercial purposes. Frank demonstrates that cool's association with rebellion and resistance to authority are often used by advertisers to make potential costumers feel that they, too, are being rebellious when they purchase a given product. Frank writes, "Commercial fantasies of rebellion, liberation, and outright 'revolution' against the stultifying demands of mass society are commonplace almost to the point of invisibility in advertising, movies, and television programming" (4). In particular, Frank shows that the language of the 1960s counterculture provided advertisers with a plethora of material for making shoppers feel rebellious in their purchasing habits. While mainstream American culture may have found the ideas of such 1960s figures as the Beatnik writers, LSD guru Timothy Leary, and the followers of Woodstock to be in opposition to American ideals, advertisers found these vary ideals (independence, rebellion, social change) conducive to selling products. Advertisers saw in these ideals a common thread within American culture: the desire to be cool.

An example of Frank's description of cool can be seen in contemporary advertising. Clothestime, a retailer of women's apparel, offers a rebate card under the slogan "Now Getting Carded Is Cool." This rebate "card" gets stamped with every purchase of $20 or more at regional Clothestime stores. After six stamps, customers get a free T-shirt. As the Clothestime ad demonstrates through its slogan, though, to be cool is to go against the norm, to be outside of society, to transgress, or at least to present the image of transgression even if transgression does not occur. The rhetoric of the ad asks you to "get carded," to challenge the rules of purchasing goods normally not allowed to teenagers. For, after all, "getting carded" typically applies to those who are under 21 and who want to purchase cigarettes or alcohol. If you "get carded," you must be attempting to break the law regarding the purchase of such items. The Clothestime advertisement removes rebellion from a teenage context and packages it for sale. Clothestime asks consumers to think of shopping as a rebellious act that, therefore, is cool.

Likewise, the .TV Web hosting service's commercials highlight the word cool in a similar manner. .TV sells space on its computer servers so that people can create their own Web pages. But as we saw in the first chapter, Internet culture often utilizes cool for promotional purposes. One .TV television ad presents a series

**Clothestime: Getting Carded Is
Cool. Shopping as rebellion.**
Source: Used with permission of Clothestime.

of "cool" and "not cool" images over the soundtrack of Johann Strauss' "Blue Danube"; only instead of being an instrumental, the repetition of the word cool replaces the song's rhythm. Another .TV advertisement features a shirtless James Dean promoting the company's product to either a young audience or an older audience with memories of 1950s films. "James Dean was cool," the ad points out. "There was no cooler name than James Dean." After several images of Dean posing with his shirt off, the commercial concludes with the statement, "This moment of cool was brought to you by .TV."

James Dean starred in three important 1950s movies: *East of Eden*, *Rebel Without A Cause*, and *Giant*. Since Dean's death, and because of the types of characters he portrayed in these films, he has become an American pop culture icon signifying teenage rebellion. His image functions rhetorically; various interests borrow it in order to make their points. In the .TV advertisements, Dean the actual person is replaced by Dean the name. In turn, this name symbolizes rebellion. Today, Dean's image means more to us than his real life characteristics and habits. We no longer think of James Dean as the person who was born in Indiana and who died in a tragic car crash. Instead, we think of the image of Dean captured in the characters he played, a figure rebelling against parents and school. Overall, this is true for most popular culture figures. We lose touch with their real lives in favor of their image.

Go online and see for yourself the .TV advertisements (http://www.tv/en-def-26ddeec65bfe/en/press/press_ads.shtml). Do these ads do a good job persuading you via James Dean and other images? Do you get a feeling of "cool" from these ads?

.TV appropriates the image of a mythical American figure. Dean, who made only three movies in his brief career, has taken on a role beyond that of actor. His image exemplifies the universal rebel. The popular perception of Dean as indifferent, unconcerned with either personal relationships or meaningful work strengthens this advertisement. .TV asks that you:

- Be a rebel and choose .TV over other Web hosting providers who are too mainstream for cool people.
- In choosing .TV, allow yourself to be indifferent to the hype of the Internet, which is overloaded with unnecessary gadgets and gimmicks. .TV provides the "true" Web hosting experience, one free of the bothersome advertisements and promotions packaged with other services.

From the .TV example, we can make several observations:

- Attitudes are important in cool writing. Tapping into popular attitudes and belief systems can guide the writing process. When these attitudes match popular figures, we can use the figures' images in new, innovative ways in order to get our ideas across.
- What other attitudes do you think function similarly? .TV taps into rebellion. What kinds of attitudes do advertisements you are familiar with work from? Construct a list of such attitudes and advertisers that you might use later for a class assignment asking you to think about the relationship between commercials and youth cultures.

Cool Figures as Cool Writing: The Icon

We can visualize .TV as a place where the cool figure, James Dean, becomes a cool form of writing. To make this move, we have to consider how, via advertisements like .TV's, James Dean is no longer a person but an icon. An icon is a representation of a larger idea, person, or object. Icons are symbols that stand for what they replace. Computer operating systems like Windows or the Mac OS place icons on the computer's desktop to represent the programs they open. McDonald's or Burger King create iconic representations of their restaurants by using the symbols of the Golden Arches or the hamburger to create an identification with the food they sell. Sports teams place iconic representations of themselves on their clothes, often in the shape of a mascot or a letter of the alphabet that the team's name begins with. We encounter icons regularly in our daily lives.

We call celebrities icons when they achieve a certain status within the culture that aligns them with an ideal. James Dean's iconicity usually signifies rebellion. We can construct a short list of other celebrity icons and what they represent:

- Howard Stern—outrageousness
- Madonna—the true feminist
- Biggie Smalls—the gangsta
- Michael Jackson—the child at heart
- Oprah Winfrey—reading

Media representations of cool depend, to a large extent, on the ability to write with icons. Icons are easy to identify with and remember. The icon also serves as a way to facilitate brand name recognition. We recognize James Dean the icon even if we have never seen a James Dean movie. Similarly, we know the name Elvis even if we've never heard an Elvis song. Most of us can identify Elvis' name with either the figure in a leather jacket and greased hair singing and performing in the 1950s or with the overweight Vegas singer of the 1970s in a rhinestone jumpsuit.

Eventually, we stop discussing the real-life figure and begin using the icon of the figure to express other ideas. Like Dean, Elvis' iconic status in American culture transforms him from a cool figure to a cool writing form. In this way, the icon becomes an important part of cool writing. Because of the instant name and visual recognition the icon creates, the most obvious place for this kind of cool writing is in advertising. And like Dean, Elvis is often a popular choice for advertisers because of the cultural associations he carries. Recent advertisements by Energizer and Lipton Iced Tea have employed Elvis' image to sell their services. We'll return to how icons function as writing in the final chapter of this book. For now, we'll examine the relationship between icons, advertising, and the World Wide Web.

Selling the Icon

The goal of most advertising is to make the customer identify with the product on a personal level. In the 1990s, Gatorade promoted its drink with the slogan, "Be Like Mike." The idea behind the ad was that to be like basketball star

Michael Jordan, one should drink Gatorade, Jordan's preferred drink. Sometimes companies do this by identifying the product with a celebrity name; other times they do so through the company's own iconic status. Advertisers create consumer identification with products by packaging companies' goods as icons. The purpose is to replace the generic name (for example, a soft drink or a sneaker) with a brand name captured in a symbolic representation. Nike, for example, uses the symbol of the swoosh to represent its footwear. Mercedes Benz, Apple Computers, and Adidas all have created brand names for themselves via the persistent display of their company icons. The way we identify with these icons says a great deal about our relationship to consumer culture and to cool.

- Make a list of icons that immediately come to mind. They can be company icons or celebrity icons. What ideals do you typically associate with these representations? Discuss as a class how we come to associate a given ideal with an icon.
- What cultural assumptions and backgrounds do we draw upon to make such associations? Do icons play off of our previous knowledge and experience? How?

The Example of Nike

If we want to describe iconic writing (using the icon to express an ideal or statement), the shoe company Nike provides a good example of how the icon is used as a cool method of expression. When we discuss commercial examples like Nike, we're not criticizing the company, but merely using it as an example. Don't interpret the example as an endorsement or critique of the company's practices or products.

In the spring of 2001, Nike's Web page (http://www.nike.com) featured a collage juxtaposing their product with a popular culture celebrity, former Sacramento Kings and current Memphis Grizzlies point guard Jason Williams. Basketball fans visiting the site could quickly recognize Williams even though his face has been cropped out of the page. The only thing visible was Williams' upper body. For basketball fans, the prominent display of Williams' tattoos on his arm acted as a reminder of who the site featured. Fans can recognize that these are Williams' tattoos. In addition, the tattoo itself also is iconic; it functions as an iconic representation of an ideal Williams had permanently written onto his body.

Williams appears as the cool figure. He is quick and athletic, and his no-look passes demonstrate indifference to other players on the court. His tattoos belong to a long tradition of cool figures who tattoo themselves with various marks (basketball star Allen Iverson also tattooed most of his body; former basketball star Dennis Rodman has numerous tattoos). Viewers of this site, however, were asked to make an immediate association between Williams' cool traits and Nike's cool product. Several of the company's products were on display next to Williams. Like the .TV commercial, Nike suggested that to be cool like Williams, one needs to wear Nike's apparel (as opposed to getting a tattoo).

Nike's lesson for cool writing involves a method for displaying iconic images in a persuasive manner. When this page was online (Nike changes its Web site on a regular basis), viewers could see the prominent display of the Nike swoosh in the upper left-hand corner of the site. Strategically placed below the swoosh, new designs of the Nike sneaker were featured. To the right of the sneakers, Jason Williams' tattoo stood out. The counterclockwise motion of the site guided viewers to draw associations between all three images.

The overall rhetorical effect of the Nike site situates the spectator (the visitor to the site) within a series of associative iconic images. We are left identifying with both the image of the tattooed basketball star and the shoe itself. In place of Williams' face (which is not displayed), the site seems to suggest, we should place our own. In this way, we identify with Nike's product. The visual display of these various images, therefore, creates a rhetoric, a method of expression. The Nike site is an important lesson in using icons. Specific and thought-out positioning of images can have an effect on how readers react to one's work. As we use images for our Web writing, we need to keep this point in mind.

Further Reading

Espen, Hal. "Levi's Blues." *The New York Times Magazine* 21 March 1999.
Ewen, Stuart. *All Consuming Images: The Politics of Style in Contemporary Culture.* New York: Basic Books, Inc., 1984.
Savan, Leslie. "Niked Lunch: Ads From the Underground." *Village Voice* 6 September 1994.

Web Site

On *Writing About Cool's* Web site, you can find more information regarding the ways advertising appropriates cool figures like Kurt Cobain or James Dean. You can also find links to additional Web sites which use the icon as a way to write as well as additional ideas regarding your own ability to write with icons.

Class Discussion

1. We've discussed products and celebrities as icons. But can we make ourselves iconic as well? If so, how? How have you made yourself iconic in the past? Have you ever used a representation, an image, a word to stand in for you, the person?
2. As a class, create iconic representations of yourselves. Pass the icons around. See who can identify who by only the icon.
3. How do religious groups use icons? How do universities? How do cities?

Exercises: The Icon Assignment

1. Nike teaches us how to work with iconic representation. Nike is persuasive because of its usage and placement of icons. We need to keep this in mind when we look to our own writing. How can we use iconic images in hypertext? Does the icon allow us to express ourselves in ways text doesn't? Create a Web page or series of Web pages constructed only from icons so that the combined icons make a statement or express an idea. Your icons can be linked to one another or appear all at once on one page.

    You can find iconic presentations of figures, companies, ideas, and other items by using various search engines to locate such images. Instead of merely listing the images on a Web page, however, experiment with various ways to position your images. Use the online, accompanying Web site to this book or a relevant HTML guide for instruction on how to use tables. Tables will help you work with the layout of your page.

    How does a traditional written analysis differ from your iconic writing? How are using images similarly or differently than you might use words to express yourself?

2. Repeat the same exercise, only this time use only celebrity images. Accumulate as many images of one celebrity as you can find. How can you use these images to create a Web page (or series of Web pages) that argues that this particular individual represents a specific ideal (like excessiveness, feminism, patriotism, etc.)?

3. Using only icons, create a home page that describes yourself. This assignment asks you to use images and the placement of those images in such a way that your audience will understand who you are and what you stand for.

    Choose your iconic representations from the discipline you are studying, work you've done, experiences you've had, civic and religious groups you belong to, etc.

Chapter

4

Advertising and Youth Culture

Teenage Cool

As we continue to see through examples like that of Nike or the various Web sites described in the previous chapters, cool is deeply tied to consumerism. The idea of cool drives consumer culture by influencing the way product information is displayed as well as consumer spending habits. Journalist Malcolm Gladwell, for instance, has written about how this version of cool has led to the establishment of a New York group of fashion experts called "the coolhunters."

Gladwell's essay "The Coolhunt," which appeared in the *New Yorker* magazine in 1997, tracked the ways merchandise managers of clothing and sneaker companies (the cool hunters) discover new styles in the streets of urban cities. The Coolhunters follow teenagers around the city and take notes on how youth transform understandings of iconic commercial goods, and how they appropriate these products for their own needs. Brand names like BMX, Reebok, and Tommy Hilfiger, the coolhunters ascertain, are often adapted by teenagers and worn in ways unintended by the manufacturers. The coolhunters take special care to pinpoint how appropriation occurs among teenagers. They do so because they want to teach companies how to replicate the process on their own. In this way, street culture's unique wearing of clothes—a practice created on urban streets—determines how future products are designed and sold.

Gladwell notes that tracing the roots of fashion trends is an elusive task. Baggy jeans may be the result of kids imitating the prison look, skateboarders trying not to resemble skiers, or both. In addition, the street attitudes that create new trends may change quickly and without notice. Cool, as it is determined by consumer habits, is an ever-shifting activity, difficult to pin down, but always unproblematic to name. Teenagers know "what is cool," the theory goes, by merely examining the product. Once a jacket or pair of shoes is worn in a unique manner, they know when to label it cool and when to label it uncool.

Fashion is one of the most easily recognizable traits of cool. What clothes or accessories do you or others you know identify as markers of cool? How long do these items last as "cool" items? One year? Two years? Do you recognize the coolhunters' objectives as familiar and something you have participated in doing as well: labeling products as cool or uncool?

Media theorist Douglas Rushkoff adopts a similar position regarding the connection between youth culture and consumerism. Rushkoff's television documentary *The Merchants of Cool* examined how corporations create intricate tie-ins between their products and cool. In particular, Rushkoff paid careful attention to current music trends. He demonstrated how concerts that appear to be artistically produced are, in fact, planned and controlled by companies such as MTV and Sprite. Like Gladwell, Rushkoff draws awareness to the ways corporations create brand names out of teenage attitudes.

Rushkoff's theory isn't new. In the early days of rock and roll, the producers of music-related events understood that attitudes like cool would help sell products. Allen Freed, one of the first rock and roll DJs and the man who claimed he invented the phrase rock and roll, held large parties in the 1950s that were sponsored by major corporations like 7-Up. Freed also received payment from record companies in return for playing on the radio records those companies produced. Thus, as early as the 1950s, musical taste and consumerism were interlinked. While Rushkoff's theory simply updates an old trend among patrons and producers of popular culture, it is worth looking at more closely.

Important in Rushkoff's analysis is the continued alliance between corporate production and youth attitudes. We can extrapolate from Rushkoff several observations by briefly examining other corporate applications of cool (observations absent in Rushkoff's documentary, but important nevertheless to understanding how advertising plays off our cultural assumptions). Our doing so will give us more models to work with as we continue learning how to write cool. The idea is to learn the rhetorical lesson from business culture, how it situates popular terms for persuasive purposes. Unlike these corporations, we don't have goods to sell. But like them, we want to learn how to be persuasive in our writing. Their usage of cool presents a good model to work with.

Mazda, for instance, ran a 1998 television commercial for its Protégé model entitled "Cool World." In the commercial, a pop song-driven narrative describes several young, urban people getting into a Protégé. The song informs viewers how hip these Mazda customers are as they pop CDs into the car's player and move to the beat. Some of the lines are:

Karen dumped her boyfriend Jim
Forget that slacker misery
Charlie works in cyberspace
Backslash dot com all day long

These twenty-something consumers belong to the hip world of cyberculture. Forgetting the "slacker" moniker bestowed upon the so-called Generation Y, these individuals work in Internet-related businesses (Charlie works in cyberspace) and utilize cyberproducts (like CDs and Mazda automobiles engineered by new technology). As the commercial ends with the promise that the Protégé is "A change from all your high-maintenance relationships," consumers are tuned into a catch phrase from youth culture—high maintenance, a popular slang term signifying a relationship requiring extra attention.

Converse Sneakers also has used cool as part of the company's marketing strategy. In *Sign Wars*, a detailed analysis of advertising, Robert Goldman and Stephen Papson point out how Converse creates identification between its All-Star sneaker and cool through the "So ugly, they're cool" campaign. In the commercial, Converse labels the All-Star as cool because of the shoe's authenticity, lack of high-tech design, and emphasis on the classic canvas look. "The point is not to be beautiful," the ad's male spokesperson states. "The point is to be yourself." Once again, cool means independence, even rebellion against the glitz and glitter of luxury and accessory (like Nike's pump).

Goldman and Papson also remind readers that this rhetorical move has been carried out by other companies, notably Sprite. In one Sprite commercial, a young male figure engages with his inner voice. His inner voice asks him, "What is cool? Does who ya hang with make you cool?" After questioning whether or not specific groups of young people are cool (skateboarders, preppies, hip-hop fans), the answer is "Give your brain a rest. Obey your thirst."

Each of these advertising examples reveals a pattern: Words associated with attitude can be used in persuasive ways. What other words could substitute for cool in these ads? And if not in ads, then, in what other media (political speech, academic essay, newscast, etc.)?

Like Converse, Sprite's message is be cool, be your own boss, be independent, don't follow rules. For Rushkoff, such attitudes are at the heart of cool and youth culture, for they always contradict one another. We, potential consumers, are asked to be independent, yet we are also asked to comply with the commercial's main objective: buy this product.

Just as important for Rushkoff is how Sprite fashions itself into an icon, even as it claims it does otherwise. Sprite's Web site (http://www.sprite.com) asks: "Want cool deals?" and responds by reminding its viewers to search out "the latest and greatest deals" from the company's Web partners like Urbanwhere.com. Urbanwhere, a clothing retailer, features "the latest urban fashions" straight from the streets of New York City. Amid such partnerships and a backdrop of images meant to signify walls spray-painted with graffiti, Sprite's Web site declares itself as street-savvy, as being down with hip-hop culture and all that it entails; i.e., Sprite is cool. In this way, Sprite utilizes the practice of juxtaposition: bringing together unlike items in order to create a new image. The juxtaposition of a soft drink with the urban street makes us think that an association exists between the two items. Because of this association, Sprite hopes we will drink its product in order to feel that we are street-wise and street hip.

- Sprite teaches us another method for cool writing: the juxtaposition of unlike items creates in us very powerful associations.
- Find a number of images. Experiment by juxtaposing them in a variety of ways. One way to do so is by using image rollovers; you can go to this book's Web site for additional information on how to make an image rollover. How many ways can you combine several images to make a multitude of points?

On television, Sprite produces advertisements claiming its own name as iconic. "Image is nothing," the ads declare, "Thirst is everything." At the heart of this slogan, the viewer is supposed to believe that Sprite cares little for image. Of course, if that were the case, why would the company need a television ad? Sprite's purpose, like any other producer of consumer goods, is to create a brand name, much in the way that James Dean or Madonna have become brand names both in popular culture as well as within the products that carry these artists' images. Even though Sprite alleges it wants potential customers to think image matters little to the company's success, the use of elaborate imagery remains present in Sprite's media productions. Thus, Sprite becomes iconic even as it declares its intentions otherwise. In this sense, like the previous Converse and Sprite examples, cool involves contradiction and paradox when applied to consumer culture.

Visit Sprite's Web site devoted to the "obey your thirst" campaign (http://www.sprite.com/thirst) or watch its archived videos of commercials featuring basketball star Kobe Bryant (http://www.sprite.com/air/kobe). Note the way Sprite combines the rhetoric of rebellion and individuality with consumerism.

All in all, even careful analysis of cool as cultural phenomenon doesn't escape the draw of marketing and consumerism. While Rushkoff's depiction of cool levels a warning against the exploitation of teenagers by major companies, the Web site companion to his show, hosted by PBS at http://www.pbs.org/wgbh/pages/frontline/shows/cool/, carries a banner above every page with several options—to search PBS' main Web site, to check out PBS' local programming schedule, and to shop. The show is for sale, and maybe in the near future related products will be as well. What we see in Rushkoff's study is a return to where we began. Cool and the Web continue to join together through consumerism. One would think that such relationships are unbreakable. Yet there exist certain groups dedicated to breaking such bonds. In the next chapter, we'll learn how those groups use writing in order to do so.

Further Viewing

The Merchants of Cool. Prod. Douglas Rushkoff. Dir. Goodman Barak. Frontline, 2001.

MTV's popular show *Total Request Live,* hosted by Carson Daly, deals with the same issues that Rushkoff's documentary and Sprite's Web site do. They balance the influence of corporate needs and teenage tastes. Viewers call in and request their favorite videos. Commentary by the show's host is often intertwined with advertisements. Videos also function as advertisements; they encourage viewers to buy the CDs on which the songs can be heard.

Further Reading

Gladwell, Malcolm. "The Coolhunt." *The New Yorker* 17 March 1997.

"Stuffing MTV's Ballot Box." Article on Salon.com, an online magazine dealing with cultural and political issues. http://www.salon.com/tech/feature/2001/08/28/trl/. The article questions the relationship between musical taste and corporations, examining problems with the voting on MTV's *Total Request Live*.

Who Owns What. http://www.cjr.org/owners/index.asp. An online source for figuring out the complex relationships between companies.

Web Site

On this book's Web site, you'll find more information about how MTV uses teenage attitudes to sell music and related products.

Class Discussion

1. Talk about the commercials you enjoy watching. Which ones resemble our discussion in this chapter?
2. How often do you watch MTV or another music channel? Have you ever participated in the voting process for your favorite video? Discuss why you want to vote for a video or song.
3. What videos do you see on MTV? Are there videos that the channel never shows? Which ones? Why? How does MTV's financial relationship to record companies influence its decision to show videos? Did MTV always play the kinds of musical videos it plays today? When did it first start playing videos by African-American artists? Why do you think it started doing so?
4. Is there a rhetoric to fashion? Do specific clothes or brand names carry rhetorical meanings?

Exercises: Adventures in Advertising, Part I

1. The relationship between performers, the places where we listen to and watch performers, and corporations is a very tight one whose bonds are not always apparent. This exercise asks you to think about the chapter's discussion regarding corporate influence in order to create your own analysis.

   MTV's popular show *Total Request Live* gave band Limp Bizkit their first real success by making their music number one on the show's listings. The show's viewers requested Limp Bizkit's songs, and MTV, in turn, played the song's videos.

The company that produces Limp Bizkit's music is called Interscope. Interscope is owned by the larger media company Time Warner. Is there a relationship between MTV and Time Warner? Is it possible that viewers didn't vote Limp Bizkit number one on *Total Request Live*, but that corporate influence had a role in the musician's popularity? The entertainment industry is, in fact, a relatively small industry. Research the major entertainment companies (Disney/ABC, AOL/Time Warner, Viacom/CBS, etc.), and see how few they are in number.

Using hyperlinks, map out the various relationships among these major companies. Allow your links to show not only the relationships that exist, but also examples of the companies' products and where these products sometimes intersect with one another in various venues (television, movies, music). Your project should use hyperlinks to demonstrate the intricate relationships between companies.

2. Create a second Web site that argues that one word unifies all of these sites' promotional activities. For theorists like Rushkoff, that word is cool. But is it the only one? Examine the patterns within your first site (the repetition of similar ideas, themes, words, products) and identify one word that either repeats itself or describes the pattern that repeats.

Then construct an argument that this word is representative of commercial interaction with media culture.

Chapter

Resistance to Advertising: The Cool Approach

So far, we've seen how advertisers appropriate teenage attitudes related to cool in order to market commercial products. In this chapter, we'll learn more about advertising methods in order to generalize from such methods applications that are relevant to our own writing. We aren't going to learn how to be advertisers; instead, we'll use advertising (and antiadvertising) to learn rhetorical strategies that are applicable to the work we do in hypertext.

Advertising notices how teenagers quickly identify their own attitudes (rebellion, for example) with a product. Borrowing from the work of cultural critic Louis Althusser, we can call this process *interpellation*. Althusser created the notion of interpellation in order to explain how groups (schools, governments) or media (advertisements, television) encourage us to identify with specific ideas. Groups and media forms "hail" us; that is, they call to us in inviting ways. In particular, interpellation involves how these groups force us to identify with their beliefs in ways we don't realize. The process of interpellation, then, is a subtle one; its purpose is to create identification that appears "natural." We don't challenge how our identities are shaped by outside forces because we're not aware that the process is occurring.

Sprite provides a good example of this process in action. Sprite asks that we "obey our thirst." The implication of this slogan is that we be ourselves when choosing a soft drink; we shouldn't follow the lead of a marketing campaign. Sprite "hails" us into thinking we are independent thinkers when we enter the marketplace. We consider our purchases as resulting from the "freedom of choice" we typically associate with buying products and services. Yet, even when Sprite encourages us to "obey our thirst," they are really asking us to be Sprite consumers and buy their product. Choice, therefore, is not an issue. As smart shoppers, we notice the contradiction, but often we still buy the product anyway.

Sprite's slogan plays off cultural values. Teenagers often ask the same thing: let me be myself, let me dress as I want, let me associate with whom I want, let me listen to whatever music I want. The results of such behavior are mine and mine alone. Teenagers, however, forget that their decisions are always framed within the greater family and society rules and norms they follow. The teenager who invokes a cool attitude—let me do what I want to do—is caught in a system where his or her parents buy the clothes, pay the bills, pay rent, etc. The option for free choice is limited. The Sprite slogan resembles this contradiction.

Think of how many popular songs play into this way of thinking. Which ones tell us to be ourselves while, at the same time, they "hail" us into performing a specific behavior?

Make a list of the things you believe you are free to do or choose. Then interrogate your own list. What constraints are you forgetting? What factors are you leaving out that may limit your ability to choose or do something?

Sprite identifies itself with typical teenage attitudes. Using cool to sell a product creates an identification between the customer and the product, an identification that tells the customer, "I am cool because I've made this purchase." Such identifications blur the boundaries between our consumption habits and our daily lives. We begin to think less about why we consume. Instead, we buy products merely because we identify with them. By enforcing this identification, many advertisers undermine the uniqueness of cool; they reduce cool to a ploy, a trick to convince youth to purchase items they might not necessarily need or want. Teenage notions of cool become appropriated for economic reasons.

Appropriation, however, doesn't always have to be a marketing strategy. Appropriation can be used for any number of purposes, from supporting a dominant way of thinking to undermining it. In this way, appropriation acts as an excellent writing strategy. Advertising, in some ways, supports the dominant way of thinking; it reinforces popularly held beliefs regarding consumption and economics. For the most part, American culture is a consumer culture. Good or bad, advertising taps into our shopping habits, wants, and desires. When we feel overwhelmed by advertising's efforts, we can think of appropriation alternatively as a model for redirecting advertisers' methods. This position doesn't state that advertising is a "bad" practice. But it does offer appropriation as a method for countering the powerful control advertising tends to have over us.

Advertising's usage of appropriation can be directed at the advertisers themselves; that is, we can appropriate their images and slogans for substituted intentions. By doing so, we see that appropriation can teach a resistance strategy applicable to our writing. If advertising methods seem to be overpowering, we can reapply the concept of appropriation to regain some of that power. When we discuss the relationship between cool and literature, we'll see this approach to appropriation again. For now, we can look at how specific groups attempt to resist the lure of advertising through appropriation. By examining these groups, we will discover rhetorical models for our own writing. The idea is not just to imitate these models, but to learn approaches that can be generalized to work we do for our classes and elsewhere.

Cultural Jamming

Media theorist Mark Dery calls the appropriation of advertising slogans and images for resistance purposes "cultural jamming." Cultural jamming, Dery states, is itself appropriated from a 1970s CB term for illegal interruptions in CB and radio broadcasts. When CB and radio transmissions came under attack by strange sounds and noises, they were being "jammed" by users attempting to break up communication. Dery notes how "jamming" no longer refers only to radio broadcast transmissions, but rather to efforts to undermine specific cultural practices. Dery, a long-time member of The Well community, sees current cultural jamming as a grass roots organization intent on taking back media forms for non-commercial purposes. Proponents of cultural jamming target advertising which has been deemed abusive or misleading. Dery believes cultural jamming is a way to empower everyday citizens so that they can voice alternative ideas regarding consumerism and governmental control.

In an often cited essay entitled "Cultural Jamming: Hacking, Slashing, and Snipping in the Empire of Signs" (http://www.levity.com/markdery/culturjam. html), Dery traces the notion of cultural jamming to a variety of cultural practices that have attempted to resist commercial and political influence in our daily lives: the French Situationist art movement of the late 1950s and 1960s, the photomontage artists of Germany before and during World War II, and the work of author William S. Burroughs (who we'll discuss at greater length in the literature section). All of these groups/writers discovered that media forms can be reworked for purposes unintended by their original producers. They sought out alternative methods for critiquing media and commercial production, but they chose to do so by recontextualizing the methods already employed by the very subjects they felt deserving of critique.

Search the Internet for further information regarding these figures. What exactly did the Situationists do? Who were the German photomontage artists who worked prior to and during World War II? Can you find examples of their work? What are the names of the novels William S. Burroughs wrote? What is the name of the writing strategy he invented?

Currently, we can look to the World Wide Web for two examples of contemporary cultural jammers who critique advertising. These examples give us additional models for cool writing because they place a significant amount of their writing on the Web. The first, Subvertise.org, (http://www.subvertise.org) hosts Subvertise's online efforts to resist advertising. The site explains its purpose as follows:

> Subvertising is the Art of Cultural resistance. It is the "writing on the wall," the sticker on the lamppost, the corrected rewording of Billboards, the spoof T-shirt; but it is also the mass act of defiance of a street party. The key process involves redefining or even reclaiming our environment from the corporate beast. Subvertising is a lot like good modern art—they both involve finding idiots with too much power and wealth, and taxing them.

Subvertise plays on the word subvert. Their intent is to subvert commercial advertising in order to demonstrate the sponsors' supposedly true intentions. Many of the subvertisements posted on the group's Web site are sent in by individuals angry about how advertising distorts certain ideas (like cool) for profit. One of the more prominent contributors to Subvertise is the Billboard Liberation Front, an artist group with strong political beliefs who reconstruct commercial billboards. Often, the Billboard Liberation Front rewrites actual billboards as in the critique of Apple Computers Think Different campaign shown below.

Here the phrase Apple originally used, "Think Different," is meant to encourage consumers to use Apple computers as an alternative to traditional methods of thinking. Doing so, according to Apple, will allow Apple users to "think different," as the figures displayed in the computer company's ads have done. The Billboard Liberation Front subverts Apple's slogan into "Think Disillusioned."

The Billboard Liberation Front's action prompts a number of rhetorical questions: Why did The Billboard Liberation Front alter the advertisement? What is wrong with Apple Computers? Who and what are disillusioned? These types of questions should be asked as a first step towards questioning any company or organization's purposes. The subverted advertisement doesn't address directly whether anything is wrong with Apple or not. Something about Apple Computers has created a sense of disillusionment among the subvertisers. At the very least, the reworking of the ad asks us to rethink how we respond to ads. Ads, like all

"Think Different" becomes "Think Disillusioned."
Source: Used with permission of The Billboard Liberation Front.
Photo: The Billboard Liberation Front.

forms of writing, are constructed from the writer's ideological beliefs. Ads are not innocent writings. They aim to create a response and an action.

Is there anything wrong with Apple identifying its product with individuals who supposedly have "thought different" and helped change the world? How do you respond to these ads? Are your impressions different or the same as The Billboard Liberation Front?

Do you think it's proper for The Billboard Liberation Front to deface billboards companies have paid for? Is this merely vandalism? Or would you call this a different method of critique?

In this critiqued ad, the Buddhist Tibetan religious leader the Dalai Lama is featured. Other Apple ads employ the images of Albert Einstein and Mahatma Gandhi. All of these figures are icons in contemporary culture; they have come to be associated with positive attributes for their ideas and actions. The Dalai Lama, for instance, has tirelessly led efforts to regain Tibet's independence from China. Typically, these are figures we would find appropriate for self-identification purposes. What is wrong with identifying with the Dalai Lama? If Apple desires that its product be worth consumer identification, is there anything wrong with choosing the Dalai Lama as a role model instead of an athlete, business tycoon, or a stereotypical teenager?

In response to Subvertise's critique of the appropriation of these iconic images, you might ask why Subvertise objects to and calls this kind of activity a "disillusionment."

- What is wrong with appropriating iconic figures for commercial purpose?
- Is there anything related to Apple's history or reputation that might lead to such a critique? In other words, does Apple's own iconic image contrast with its appropriation of so-called sacred figures like Gandhi or the Dalai Lama?
- Do we think that the iconic representations of these types of figures are beyond commercial usage? If yes, then why?
- Recently, a communications company reworked images from Martin Luther King's "I Have a Dream" speech, given in Washington, D.C., in 1963, in order to produce a television advertisement for its product. Is King, like the Dalai Lama, a figure we shouldn't appropriate for our writing? Why or why not? Is this a wrong usage of appropriation for rhetorical purposes? Or is it as justified as Apple's usage of the Dalai Lama?

Adbusters

The second example of culture jamming comes from Adbusters. Adbusters hosts its site at Adbusters.org (http://www.adbusters.org). Adbusters specializes in producing spoof ads. In particular, it directs specific attention to ads that highlight the concept of cool for commercial purposes. Adbusters' founder Kalle Lasn describes the group's efforts as anti-cool. For Lasn, cool creates the atmosphere conducive to advertising's aims. In her book, *Culture Jam: The Uncooling of America*, Lasn describes cool as the cornerstone of an addictive, dispensable culture concerned mostly with appearance and fashion. Lasn's version of cool concentrates on the cultural dominance of trademarks and the ways we identify with those trademarks. Gap, BMW, Nike, Marlboro—all create consumer identification, and specifically, Lasn states, elitist systems of identification that divide society into haves and have-nots. Those that can afford these products identify themselves with a consumer-oriented society; those that can't afford to buy such goods feel alienated and left out of society.

Cigarette companies are some of Adbusters favorite subjects of critique. In particular, Camel and Kool use their brand names to create consumer identification with the concept of cool. The now banned Joe Camel ads of the 1980s and 1990s attempted to make smoking cool for teenagers. Joe Camel, dressed in designer clothes, wearing dark sunglasses, and often driving a high-priced automobile, appeared cool because he smoked Camel cigarettes.

Kool, on the other hand, immediately evokes the idea of cool by its very name. Replace the "K" with a "C" and you have cool: what you will be if you smoke this brand of cigarettes. Adbusters treats Kool's "Utter Kool" campaign with its own version of what happens to smokers by changing "Utter Kool" to "Utter Fool." Go online to http://adbusters.org/creativeresistance/spoofads/tobacco/fool/ad.jpg and you will find the "Utter Fool" ad. Through appropriation, Adbusters alters Kool's attempt to align its brand name with cool. Adbusters' ad suggests smoking as foolish because of the related health dangers. The group uses a rhetoric of appropriation to critique smoking and the dangers connected with this habit.

From the prevailing theme of cool we've noticed in corporate advertising campaigns, we can name the appropriation of such ads as cool as well. To write cool in this manner is to appropriate for the purpose of critique. If you appropriate a saying, image, slogan, etc. for the purpose to create critique, you are engaging with cool writing. Critique draws attention to a common practice we often take for granted, like advertising.

- How often do we watch ads and not think about how they might be influencing our behavior?
- How easy is it for you to say, "Ads have no effect on me; I can watch them and not be influenced"?
- When we adopt this position without reflection, we are taking for granted the way media forms shape our convictions. We are *uncritically* accepting representations.

Critique opens up debate regarding common practices and allows for new opinions to form. Critique is the basis of all writing, for we use writing to express our opinions as well as to shape new beliefs. As an act of resistance, cool critique opens up new possibilities for the ways we write about and with media. Adbusters, for example, asks that consumers think beyond the image of coolness cigarette companies associate with their products and instead consider the health problems associated with smoking. Rather than write such a proclamation out as a typed essay on paper, Adbusters chooses to work within the media form of advertising by presenting their ideas as images, and, in particular, as ads.

Is this method preferable to a written essay? Such a question is a question of rhetorical choice. Whether or not you make a rhetorical choice (like should I appropriate for purposes of cool writing) depends on the situation or context in which you are writing. Depending on when you are writing and who you are writing for, ask yourself which serves a more effective critique:

- A typed essay or memo denouncing cigarette companies for hiding the dangers of smoking
- A recontextualized advertisement that shocks viewers through satire or parody

What does one do that the other doesn't? Are there instances where one form might be more effective than the other? When? Where? As a class, discuss situations in which the first form might be most appropriate and situations in which the second might be.

What kind of audience do you think Adbusters is trying to reach? Adbusters' ads tend to be one image and not a series of images. Why? Does this usage of one image catch our attention quickly? Does the usage of one image teach us something about placing images on Web pages?

If Adbusters wrote out a long memorandum stating all the scientific reasons cigarettes cause cancer, would it catch our attention in the same way? In what situations would the long essay be better and in what situations is the single image better for catching an audience's attention?

Adbusters asks that we all become critical participants in consumer culture, that we ask tough questions regarding our daily interaction with mass production. In spring 2001, Adbusters posted a culture jamming contest on its Web site (http://www.adbusters.org/campaigns/placejamming/pjcontest.html) to encourage readers to voice their opinions in creative ways. The contest, Place Jamming, asked participants to challenge urban sprawl by resisting the "economic and cultural machinery" responsible for destroying city green spaces. The contests requests that entrants create a photograph or video that:

> Let [corporations] see green. Create physical space where nature can re-enter our perception. Look around you—there are potential targets everywhere. In the concrete jungle there are nooks and crannies waiting to be planted, there are rolling lawns crying out for wildflowers.

At the very least, what cultural jamming teaches us, then, is how to appropriate in a critical manner, how to reuse the tools of mainstream ways of thinking for alternative purposes. We have learned another lesson for cool writing.

Further Reading

Althusser, Louis. "Ideology and Ideological State Apparatuses." *Lenin and Philosophy, and Other Essays*. London: New Left Books, 1971.

Dery, Mark. "Culture Jamming: Hacking, Slashing and Sniping in the Empire of Signs." Westfield, NJ: Open Magazine Pamphlet Series, 1993.

Frank, Thomas. "The Conquest of Cool." *Business Culture, Counterculture, and the Rise of Hip Consumerism*. Chicago: University of Chicago Press, 1997.

Frank, Thomas, and Matt Weiland, eds. *Commodify Your Dissent: Salvos from The Baffler*. New York: W.W. Norton & Company, 1997.

Goldman, Robert, and Stephen Papson. *Sign Wars: The Cluttered Landscape of Advertising*. New York: The Guilford Press, 1996.

Lasn, Kalle. *Culture Jam: The Uncooling of America*. New York: Eagle Brook, 1999.

Rushkoff, Douglas. *Cyberia: Life in the Trenches of Hyperspace*. San Francisco: Harper, 1994.

Films to Watch

The Merchants of Cool. Prod. Douglas Rushkoff. Dir. Goodman Barak. Frontline, 2001. As described in the previous chapter, a documentary on cool and youth culture.

Medium Cool. Dir. Haskell Wexler. Paramount Pictures, 1969. This film gives us another place to consider the media's affect on reporting, the way media alter our perceptions. Media production and its internal contradictions are the focus of this film's treatment of 1960s political events.

Web Site

In addition to the exercises below, you can find more cultural jamming influenced cool writing exercises on this book's Web site.

Class Discussion

1. Is consumerism's usage of cool a no-win situation? Are we helpless victims to advertising's manipulation of our interests? Or is there more to the picture than this?
2. Brainstorm to create a list of advertisements you think are misleading in how they redirect teenage consumers. What are their tactics? How might these goods not be attractive to teenagers without the slogans and imagery employed? Would they even be attractive at all?
3. Discuss as a class favorite brand names. Why do you like these brands? Is it their utility (i.e., their quality and usage) or something else? How has advertising led you to use these brands? Or has it?

4. Using the Internet and your library, research print advertisements and commercials that use cool to sell their products. How extensive is the list? Repeat the same process with other terms. What kind of observations can you draw from this type of research?

Exercises: Adventures in Advertising, Part II

1. Gladwell and Rushkoff see youth as a main contributor to cool as commercialism. But they also feel that the ideologies of consumerism adapt youthful attitudes for commercial purposes. Using the styles and attitudes you are familiar with in popular media forms (music, fashion, television), create your own Web version of what cool means to youth culture.

   • How much is your version dependent on commercial products (Nike, Sprite, MTV)? How much of it isn't? How do the slogans of advertising change the ways you will set up a Web site? Do they guide you? Deter you?

   • To do this project, you need to research the ways styles and attitudes are shaped by companies. Adapt these companies' approaches to create your own version of cool. Much of this will involve you imitating the companies' methods. By imitating previous methods of expression, we can learn a great deal about how to express ourselves.

2. Design a Web site for a youth-oriented audience in which you treat a political topic as if it were a fictitious product. In other words, how can you use the rhetorical lessons we've learned in this chapter to convince others to recognize your position? To do this, pick a specific issue of interest to you. Then do the following:

   • Outline a plan that will treat that issue like an advertisement. How, for example, will you present your idea? Using what strategies that companies tend to use? How will you appeal to your audience's expectations and common assumptions?

   • Much of what we see advertisers do involves tapping into popular assumptions and beliefs. How can you do the same?

   • How do the lessons of Nike (in Chapter 3) and Sprite motivate and inspire your work? Why do they? How can you work with icons the way Nike does? Can you strategically place images in order to create a statement? Using icons (no words), can you create a site that persuades viewers to listen to your ideas? Or, like Sprite, can your site use short, fragmented phrases juxtaposed with other items not typically associated with your topic (the way Sprite puts its soft drink amid an urban backdrop)? Like both, can you appropriate ideas from other cultural groups and use them as part of your argument?

3. Adopt the method of appropriation endorsed by Subvertising and Adbusters to create your own cultural critique. Find an advertisement that you feel hides an important message (either because of the dangers of its product or because of the way it represents a certain group of people, like women, African-

Americans, Hispanics, or others). Then use hypertext (and if available a graphic manipulation program) to rework the ad.

- Why did you choose to critique this ad?
- How do you turn the ad back on itself? What parts of the original ad should you leave in place so that your audience recognizes what you are critiquing? What should you alter?
- Could you use a series of hyperlinks to get your readers to click through various pages, each leading up to the critique? Could you use more advanced hypertextual features to change the nature of the ad? Features like rollovers, the refresh tag, or pop-up windows can create alternative viewpoints that juxtapose with the original ad. On this book's Web site there are links to various online resources where you can find easily accessible code to cut and paste for your own usage.

4. Do the same kind of critique for a Web site you've visited. Keep in mind that Internet browsers have an option called "View Source" or "Page Source" which allows you to look at a particular Web site's HTML code. Sometimes it's too difficult to figure out how a Web site is constructed, but usually you can use this option as part of your appropriative strategy. In order to critique a Web site by jamming it, you can use the site's code and fill in your own content. This is, in essence, Adbusters' strategy when it takes over an ad. It adopts that ad's original look and alters it as part of the critique.

5. Do the same thing with a political speech or statement. The techniques of Subvertising and Adbusters can also be used to critique political leaders, ideas, or movements. Use recent political statements or older, well-known statements (such as John F. Kennedy's famous inaugural speech: "Ask not what your country can do for you, but what you can do for your country"). Think of how you approached the previous assignment with Web sites. Can you do the same again?

6. Go even further in your cool, appropriative critiques. Create a Subvertise/Adbuster styled critique of these very organizations we're learning from. Can you offer insight into issues at stake in these group's activities? Are they beyond critique?

Chapter

6

Culture

Through the first five chapters of this book, we have seen how advertising and economic interests use cool in various ways, usually as a method for turning an emotional value into a commercial interest. This chapter continues the previous chapters' discussions within the context of culture. As you may remember from the Introduction, a central component of this book's focus includes addressing the aims of cultural studies. Implicit in those aims is the study of culture. What we mean by the word culture, though, includes a variety of definitions which at times complement one another, contradict one another, and overlap with one another. In essence, we use the word culture the way we've been using and will continue to use the word cool.

What is culture? How do you define culture? Does culture indicate the things we own, the language we use, the places we work and study, entertainment, literature? Would you include television shows in your definition? Would you include poetry? What about toys? Is there such a thing as "American culture"? Or does there exist more than one thing we might identify as "American culture"?

This chapter doesn't attempt to answer any of these questions, but it does want to put all of these questions up front as we examine how cool fits into this discussion. Where does cool come from? How has it been absorbed into our daily lives? Why has it become a dominant term, a word so popular and identifiable that most people have some kind of definition of what it means? Why is it a cultural phenomenon?

Do a search on Google or Yahoo for the word "culture." How many different versions of the term appear? How have you used the word culture? How have you seen others—either people or media forms—use this term? Why are there so many discrepancies in its usage?

What does it mean to be cultured or to have culture? What is "high brow" or "low brow" culture? Where does cool usually fit in these two categories?

In this chapter, we'll examine how cool works as a culturally constructed term. What we mean by "culturally constructed" is that numerous influences shape ideas; they don't emerge from a vacuum. Instead, ideas are formed within the culture by a variety of forces (religions, media, literature, government) even if we disagree on what culture exactly entails. Racism, for example, is a culturally constructed attitude that prevails when racial groups are consistently depicted in demonizing ways. If newspapers, TV shows, films, and books all treat a specific racial group as inferior, eventually a significant number of people will believe that these images represent a reality. That reality, we can say, is a culturally constructed one. It only exists through the ways it is depicted.

- Make a list of items you believe belong within the generalized term culture.
- What influences (what you've read, watched, heard, or discussed) lead you to label these items as culture?
- Is it possible that someone else might claim that these items should not be identified as culture? Why? Who might say that?

In this chapter, we'll examine how cool is culturally constructed, and in particular, we'll study how it becomes caught between minority and majority discourses, often serving both sides' interests differently. The word discourse means, in its most basic terms, expression. We have a general method of expression that we recognize by language familiarity (we might all speak English or Spanish, for example). But we also have other means of expression that might be particular to specific interest groups (like accountants, doctors, or teachers), with specific vocabularies that are difficult for outsiders to understand. For example, the government has its own form of discourse. Reading an IRS form can be quite confusing for those who don't recognize all of the terminology. Getting a parking fine paid or waived can also be difficult for those who don't know how to speak with government clerks. Figuring out various laws and bylaws might be an insurmountable feat for those with no training in the language of law.

We refer to powerful forms of expression as *dominant* forms of discourse. These are forms of expression that have control over the way we live and think. Laws can be considered a form of dominant discourse. Specific laws restrict what we can say about other people, how fast we can drive, when we can possess a firearm, at what age we can smoke or drink, and other rules. Advertising also represents a form of dominant discourse, as we've seen. Ads exert control over our spending habits. Typically, they do so by appealing to our emotions and desires, by overlaying their discourse over our own. Think specifically about advertisements and commercials that address you, the viewer, directly in this manner:

- Sometimes you feel like a nut; sometimes you don't—Almond Joy
- Just Do It—Nike
- Have It Your Way—Burger King
- Obey Your Thirst—Sprite

- Let your fingers do the walking—Yellow Pages
- Be all you can be—The Army
- Be Like Mike—Gatorade

These examples are consumer driven. Sometimes, however, the dominant discourse is a racially motivated form of expression. In this way, the dominant discourse affects our lives because of how it describes or discriminates against our racial or ethnic makeup. Prior to Civil Rights legislation of the 1960s, white Americans controlled expression almost entirely. The rights of African-Americans were severely limited and their access to the tools for producing expression (owning newspapers, magazines, TV stations, radio stations) was also limited by prevailing discrimination policies. African-Americans, then, occupied the position of the minority discourse. Their voices were severely limited, as were many other groups including women, Native Americans, Hispanics, and homosexuals.

> Do some research on the kinds of television and film roles typically associated with various ethnic groups. What kind of patterns do you find? Are these images products of a dominant or minority discourse? The key is in figuring out who produced the discourse, not who is represented in it.

Think of the "Whites Only" signs that proliferated throughout the South up until the 1954 Supreme Court ruling in Brown v. Board of Education that separation is not equal. Who would have controlled the making and positioning of these signs? Think of the laws that dictated where African-Americans could sit on buses, what water fountains they could drink from, and what schools they could attend. Who would be the dominant force in such activity? Who made these rules? We can debate how much of contemporary American discourse is still controlled by white (often male) Americans, but we have seen some change since the 1960s. And yet, the issue of who controls how information is created and distributed still remains important.

In this chapter, we'll examine how both majority and minority discourses use cool as a means of expression. In particular, we'll look closely at the role certain parts of African-American culture play in the discourse of cool. This chapter will outline various African-American positions regarding cool, its origins, what it means, and its effect on discourse. In other words, this chapter will discuss a particular cultural effect on rhetoric. In the end, we'll use the ideas we discover in order to write electronically. The content of our study will inform the ways we write in hypertext. Just as culture affects cool, so does cool affect hypertext.

The Cultural Origins of Cool

In the early 1960s, anthropologist Robert Farris Thompson spent time researching Yoruban culture in West Africa. Examining Yoruban language and customs, Farris Thompson discovered that the Yoruban word *itutu* means the same thing as the American term cool. As employed in Yoruban culture, *itutu* represented the virtues of calmness, conciliation, and appeasement. Much in the way that "to be cool" today can mean being calm and lacking response, *itutu* operated as a word in everyday and religious expression. Cool marked a sense of lifestyle. It governed behavior and social relationships. In addition, Farris Thompson noticed that when Yorubans attempted to put the feeling of *itutu* down in a written form, they chose highly visual and graphic media over the usage of alphabetic expression. In this sense, cool acted as a form of visual writing often appearing in sculptures, textiles, and other artistic endeavors.

Farris Thompson's discovery is important for three main reasons:

- It positions cool as more than just emotion or style; cool is a way of writing.
- It identifies this form of writing as *visual*, instead of alphabetic.
- It acknowledges the cultural heritage of cool, tracing the word to African culture.

The first points reinforce the need to consider cool as a visual writing practice (i.e., writing for the Web). The last point teaches us how to forge connections between everyday language and historical meaning. Strong rhetorical possibilities exist in such acts. An exercise at the end of this chapter will ask you to consider how a historical connection to an everyday word legitimizes that word's meaning for people previously not interested in its usage. Do historical connections encourage readers to pay more attention to an initial claim? Does cool's rich African history now make it a legitimate area of study (compared to your previous conception of the term as a way to describe a pair of sneakers or a song)?

Because cool's origins can be placed within African history, its movement to America most likely came with the slave trade. Thus, cool can be examined, to some extent, as it exists within African-American culture. To understand cool's cultural significance, we need to think about its African-American heritage as well. Why must we place cool within the context of African-American culture? Does it matter if cool maintains links to non-Caucasian influences? After all, isn't this just a word everybody today uses, regardless of race? Why talk about race at all when discussing a subject like cool?

To answer these questions, we must acknowledge how everyday words maintain histories and meanings that extend beyond their everyday usage. We must be open to the possibilities that words contain rich legacies and complex backgrounds, which if exposed, might alter our assumptions and perceptions. Why, then, do we need to alter our perceptions? Sometimes our understanding of the world is slighted because of the cultural influences that interact with our daily lives. It remains important to investigate the various cultural interactions that occur in language, in work, in study, and in other activities. In turn, we allow ourselves the opportunity to learn about how and why we think the way we do.

If we never changed our way of thinking, we most likely would still think the world is flat, the sun revolves around the earth, and many other notions we have since dispelled as untrue. Yet these notions once held power over how people conceptualized their lives because of specific cultural influences like the church.

One area in which we constantly feel the pressure to reconsider our previous thinking is race.

This chapter seeks to begin the process of challenging our assumptions about race regarding words, like cool, which we take for granted as natural. Quite often, this means asking difficult questions about ourselves, the way we respond to and behave with others, and the ideas we've cherished for some time as fixed and concrete. We'll do so by looking at:

- Cool's political background
- Cool's male perspective (and lack of female representation)
- Cool's overall cultural prevalence

The purpose of this chapter, as well as that of the following chapters, is to demonstrate how cool is as much a cultural phenomenon as is any other factor. We want to learn from its cultural attributes lessons we can then take with us when we attempt to write electronically. In this way, we are trying to make connections between our cultural interests and writing.

African-American Cool

In the 1960s, America marked a moment of civil unrest. Long denied access to white America's places of entertainment, schools, methods of information dispersion, and political system, African-Americas accelerated their protest against racist oppression by demanding that these locked doors be opened to all people. The work of Martin Luther King, Jr., and Malcolm X toward obtaining racial equality is important in considering how African-American culture struggled to secure a legitimate place within white America. Each stressed a different approach to balancing power between whites and blacks; King rallied for the cause of nonviolence, and Malcolm X urged America to change "By any means necessary." Both leaders have since become cultural icons, representations of the pursuit of equality.

Another important writer to emerge in the 1960s in relation to civil rights was the poet and playwright Amiri Baraka. Baraka, who changed his name from Leroi Jones, critiqued the relationship between mainstream white culture and African-American culture by pointing out the discrepancies between the two at the level of power.

Like Martin Luther King, Jr.'s influential essay "Letter from Birmingham Jail" or Malcolm X's stunning *The Autobiography of Malcolm X*, Baraka's book *Blues People* describes the conciliatory role forced upon African-Americans in the time period leading up to the 1960s. This role left a significant portion of the American population powerless because of racial discrimination. All three of these works speak of the lack of African-American freedom in decision making, movement, and representation, as well as the struggle to achieve parity with the rest of the country's populace.

In *Blues People*, Baraka uses music as a metaphor for the complex racial relationships between the dominant white majority and the oppressed African-American minority. Music, Baraka writes, demonstrates how oppressive relationships exist in everyday life. Baraka's focus concentrates less on what the music is about and more on how it is culturally created and heard. Baraka draws attention to the ways white culture (the dominant) often appropriates African-American forms of musical production (the minority). Because of this appropriation, Baraka notes, African-American culture maintains little to no cultural, economic, or political freedom. What begins as an African-American cultural form, Baraka claims, quickly becomes adopted by white culture. When this occurs, all connections to African-American origins are quickly erased as well.

> You'll remember that in Chapter 3 we defined appropriation in terms of how advertising reuses the word cool in a different context than it was originally intended. As we read about Baraka's interest in appropriation, notice how the word's meaning changes.

For Baraka, cool indicates the feeling experienced by African-Americans when denied the ability to participate both politically and culturally. To be cool, Baraka states, is to be:

- Detached
- Uninvolved
- Nonparticipatory

When African-American music is appropriated by white culture, Baraka claims, African-Americans have no choice but to be cool. They can't respond fittingly because they're denied the right to participate in their own musical production. In addition, they're not involved in sharing the wealth when the music sells well because little to no royalty is paid to the original performer. Therefore, African-American culture has become cool. It is detached from its own roots and representations. The popular expression "Be cool" exposes a new meaning when read against this historical background.

The examples Baraka draws from to prove his point include jazz and blues music. Popular, white jazz artists of the 1930s and 1940s often eclipsed the African-American musicians who originally recorded the music that made these performers famous. In addition, dress and attitudes created by African-American culture, like the zoot suit, pork pie hat, or phrases like daddy-o, were quickly being adapted by white teenagers, but without any recognition of where the clothes and popular sayings originated. By the 1950s and 1960s, the process continued. Blues was being overpowered by up-and-coming white rock and roll artists.

Notably, performers like Elvis Presley began recording songs that had been written and previously recorded by African-American artists, most of whom were unknown to white audiences. White-owned radio stations seldom played African-American music, and white-owned record stores sold some, but not many, African-

American records. All of this exemplified the cool position afforded to African-American culture, as Baraka defines it. Although they often created the music, fashions, and language popular in mainstream culture, the African-American versions were typically forgotten and overshadowed by newer white versions.

Baraka's examples of cool dress appropriated by white culture may be unfamiliar to you. Supplement his claim by listing those fashions popular today among one ethnic group which began as the fashion of another ethnic group. You may also want to incorporate our previous discussion of fashion and the coolhunters.

Baraka's definition of cool, then, has several levels we need to consider. If cool, as Baraka claims, is a rhetorical response to oppression, we need to break down this response in order to better understand how it can be used in our own writing:

- *The cultural level.* How important is it to give credit where credit is due? An African-American artist records a record, but because it isn't played on many radio stations, few have a chance to hear it. A white artists performs the same song, and because he's white, his song is distributed to a large number of radio stations. Many listeners now hear the song, purchase the record, and the artist makes money. To be cool at this level means not being a part of the production of culture.

  How, then, does this affect our general perception of other cultures? If we are unaware of the cultural origins of a piece of music, a book we like, a word we use, does this also affect the way we perceive other racial and ethnic groups? In other words, does this lead to an overall lack of cultural knowledge on our part as well, and thus contribute to misunderstandings and prejudice?
- *The economic level.* Because of this version of appropriation, to be cool means to be denied economic rights. Doesn't the original artist deserve money for the song? Quite often enough, however, little to no royalties were paid.

  How might cool as economic policy contribute to continued, general economic problems certain racial and ethnic groups experience? If music is only one example of economic appropriation, are there other examples in which groups are denied economic participation?
- *The political level.* Not owning the rights to one's creations also denies one the right to political access. Here, political means control. To be cool at this level indicates a lack of power, an ability to control one's place and work in society. If this is true, how can someone forced into cool at this level ever obtain a better political position? How can the other levels be dealt with if political power is also absent?

We see that cool involves various issues related to interaction and involvement. As a tool to describe the lack of cultural, economic, and political involvement, cool's meaning of detachment takes on a new importance. Our participation (or lack of participation) in these areas determines how we identify ourselves. Do we feel oppressed? Do we feel empowered? Where do we feel we belong within American society? Typically, we've used cool as an identifier of personality: he's cool or she's cool. This added element, however, shifts this perception of the word so that a cool person may also mean someone struggling to deal with cultural, economic, or political issues.

Based on this breakdown, we can consider how cool is or might be used to create complex identities. In *Blues People*, Baraka's solution for cool involves defining new terms for experience. If cool has led to oppression, Baraka writes, then a new sense of identity needs to form. How we label that new sense of identity depends on what position we hold within society. The next chapter will deal at greater length with issues of identity and cool, focusing on specific moments related to African-American identity. The question of how cool relates to African-American identity, however, can, to some extent, be generalized to other ethnic groups (including ourselves) as well. Therefore, we might ask questions along the way as to how cool might rhetorically be applied to other American experiences (even if the word cool is not used to describe these experiences). The exercises for this chapter ask you to use writing in order to work with other identity groups. These exercises show you how to use cool as a tool for making meaning. By maintaining cultural, economic, and political issues central to our writing, we can redefine both our relationships to other ethnic groups as well as our understandings of our own ethnic experiences.

Further Reading

Baraka, Amiri. *Blues People: Negro Music in White America*. New York: William Morrow and Company, 1963.

Farris Thompson, Robert. *Flash of the Spirit: African & Afro-American Art & Philosophy*. New York: Vintage, 1983.

Nakamura, Lisa, Gilbert Rodman, and Beth Kolko. *Race in Cyberspace*. New York: Routledge, 2000. A collection of essays that deals with how race and cyber-culture conflict and overlap.

Web Site

On this book's Web site, there are numerous images and representations of "cool" cultural appropriations. Check out these examples and see if you can identify how these images fit or don't fit with Baraka's definition of cool.

Class Discussion

1. Can you think of contemporary examples of what Baraka calls cool? Are his observations still relevant today? If not, why not? If so, how can you identify similar cool moments today?

2. Following Baraka's definition, have there been any recent events, locally or nationally, that we might describe as cool?

3. Today, are there other ethnic groups we might describe as cool in this way? Can you think of local ethic groups in your communities that have little or no opportunity to participate culturally, economically, or politically?
4. How does all this fit with the World Wide Web? How are racial and ethnic groups represented on the Web? How are they empowered? Who does this empowering, assuming it takes place? Are there any connections between the Web and specific racial and ethnic experiences? If so, which? As a class, identify various representations on the Web and debate their construction.

Exercises: The Cyber-Identity Assignment

1. This chapter asks you to make a connection between cool and identity via Baraka's definition. Based on this discussion, compile a survey of Web sites that deal with issues of power and race. When you use a search engine like Google or Yahoo, rather than searching only for "African-American" or "Hispanic," search also for organizations that serve these groups, such as the National Association for the Advancement of Colored People (NAACP) or the Association for the Advancement of Mexican-Americans. Also look at entertainment and community based Web sites like rapstation.com that might address social issues as well. Your lists should include official agencies, artistic enterprises, commercial groups, and political action groups, among others. Concentrate your search on an ethnic or racial group that you do not consider yourself a member of.

    Once you've compiled your list, do the following:

    • Write down your observations of these sites. How, for instance, does a site dealing with Hispanic-American identity use the Web? How does it use identity-related issues to deliver its message? What kind of images does it display? Does it appropriate images from elsewhere? What words are used to link to other sections of the site? Is there anything particularly Hispanic-American about the site? What makes it specifically Hispanic-American? Repeat these and similar observations for each site you visit.

    • Construct a Web site that is divided into separate sections representing the sites you've observed. Use tables to divide your sections. Then construct a new section for your own racial or ethnic identity. Describe your background through images and text.

    • Using hyperlinks, connect those areas you've researched and described with those you've written about yourself. Are there similarities? Differences? Where are there overlaps? Where are there conflicts? See if patterns emerge that allow you to create new connections.

    • After you have found a pattern, gave a name to this new sense of cyber-identity—the overlap between your experience and your subject of study.

2. Turn this assignment into a Web essay that explores where your own identity meets other racial and ethnic groups. In hypertext, do you see yourself at all relating to this other group? What do hyperlinks do that allow you to make new connections? Allow yourself room in your essay to reflect on the similarities and differences you discover. When you see a trait in your own identity that parallels or contrasts with another group, use hyperlinks to establish the relationship. This assignment can build off of the previous one by fully exploring the name you have attributed to the ethnic overlap you discover.

3. Farris Thompson teaches that cool's origins are in the Yoruban word itutu. For the Yorubans, itutu marked a way of visual writing. In America, cool eventually became associated with popular culture and a person's status as "in" or "worth attention." Cool became visualized (in film, on TV, on the World Wide Web), but in ways different from its original meaning.

   Choose a word specific to either an ethnic group you identify with or one associated with another ethnic group. This word can be a slang term, a word found originally in another language but now used widely in English, or something different. Research the word's origins and original applications and meanings. Then create a Web site that demonstrates how this term might now be applied to a different purpose like writing (or something else). Use visual and textual documentation to support your claim.

4. Another version of the previous assignment asks you to generalize from the example of cool and its various meanings. Instead of working with the word cool, choose one word specific to an ethnic group you identify with or one associated with another ethnic group.

   Search the Web for as many usages of this term as you can find. Then create a Web site that demonstrates this term's multiple applications by hyperlinking a series of pages, each with a citation from the original usage. You may also consider using additional hypertext applications like rollovers, pop-ups, and frames to demonstrate the term's usage. Your final site will show how the word carries a variety of meanings relevant to a variety of situations.

Chapter

7

Popular Culture and Cool

B ecause Amiri Baraka concentrates on how cool functions in music, we can use popular culture to continue discussing his ideas regarding detachment and appropriation. We'll spend considerable time throughout this book looking at popular culture, but in this chapter, popular culture presents us with an excellent forum for carefully scrutinizing Baraka's claims and applying them further to our own writing. Popular cultural is a realm in which a considerable amount of expression takes place. Most of us receive the bulk of our information through the media of popular culture: television, film, music, magazines, and the World Wide Web. Even media that we associate as beyond popular culture, like news programs, for example, have become embedded within the popular. Walter Cronkite is now a popular culture icon and not just the anchorman of the nightly news, as he was throughout the 1970s. The news format, on the other hand, is used by entertainment-based TV shows that pose as the news (*Entertainment Tonight*, *The Daily Show*, and *Inside Edition*) when, in fact, they are entertainment. We might even debate how much of the major network's nightly news programs have been transformed into entertainment, and thus popular culture.

So what is popular culture? How does it differ from the definition of culture we formed in Chapter 6? Does popular culture include all culture? Our just parts of it? Can a building be a part of popular culture (like the Empire State Building) or do only people belong in the definition of popular culture (like Michael Jordan)? And do we mean real people like actors or sports figures, or do we mean cartoon characters as well (like Homer Simpson or Mickey Mouse)?

No one definition clarifies the term popular culture. By its very name we can infer that the everyday, the ordinary, the recognizable, and the popular must fall within its boundaries. The minute we mention "popular," however, we run into trouble. Popular for whom? Isn't popularity a result of individual taste and interest? When we discuss popular culture, we must suspend our personal tastes and not let them affect our understandings of the texts we read and analyze. When we use the descriptive term "popular" to describe contemporary culture, we might not mean something popular with you, but rather a person or an item recognized by a considerable number of people. This could include everything from Shakespeare to Guns and Roses, however. Is Bugs Bunny part of popular culture? What about Harley Davidson motorcycles? Is Frank Sinatra? Martin Luther King, Jr.? Legos? A soda commercial? While we might not agree on one definition, we might say that popular culture includes the producers of and products of our everyday lives.

Such a definition includes both McDonald's (the producer) and the hamburger (the product McDonald's serves) as well as Time Warner (the producer) and Bugs Bunny (the product Time Warner produces) and Ford (the car manufacturer) and the Mustang (the car Ford makes). While a discussion of popular culture can include any number of things, in this chapter we'll continue looking closely at music because Baraka's work on cool focuses on musicians and the songs they produce.

Music as Popular Culture

As we saw, Amiri Baraka uses music as a place to critique the history of American racial relations. Unless you are a jazz and blues fan, most of the musicians Baraka discusses are not very recognizable. It's probable that you're not familiar with the music of Coleman Hawkins, Lester Young, or Dizzy Gillespie, three major jazz figures Baraka discusses. Therefore, it doesn't make sense to spend time discussing Baraka's examples. If popular culture can help us understand the intricate nature of power relationships in American culture, we need examples we can recognize.

If you have any significant interest in television, film, or music, you are familiar with many modern pop stars. Contemporary performers like Eminem, Nelly, Prince, Missy Elliott, and Madonna have earned considerable financial success recording popular music. Local radio stations as well as television stations like MTV, VH1, and BETV play their music on a rotating basis, thus offering widespread exposure to their recordings. If you are a fan of their music (or of others), you might initially label their albums as cool. This song sounds great; it's cool.

Discussing music often becomes a difficult task because such conversations tend to fall back on the definition of cool as personal taste. If you say a song is cool, you are expressing your personal likes. Taste in itself doesn't spark much discussion or thought because of the difficulty in refuting someone else's likes or dislikes. This chapter asks you to put aside your tastes momentarily. We might discuss musical styles you don't like. Don't let that discourage you from thinking about the general issues at stake. While the musical styles presented here are done so for a specific reason, their attributes no doubt can be generalized to other forms you either prefer or are more familiar with. We encourage you to make those kinds of connections and to highlight them in class discussions. Remember, our purpose is to learn how these musical styles rhetorically construct meaning and how we can use these lessons to write for the Web.

Hip-Hop

We will discuss hip-hop in greater detail in Chapter 13, but in this chapter hip-hop provides an excellent example of how appropriation's relationship to music has changed since Baraka's work on cool. Baraka worried about the dominant discourses' usage of appropriation to oppress minority discourse. By using cultural production without historical context, Baraka worried that appropriation would eliminate African-American voice. With hip-hop, the rules have changed somewhat. New applications of appropriation occur in which questions of cultural oppression become minimized. In hip-hop, DJs and producers have created a new method of writing dependent on sound appropriation. They borrow extensively from prerecorded sounds and music to form new compositions. This chapter won't offer a comprehensive history of hip-hop. Instead, by looking closely at how hip-hop functions as a form of writing, we will also see how hypertext works similarly and thus encounter new instructions for hypertext writing.

Throughout the 1970s, DJs threw block parties for residents of New York's Bronx and inner city neighborhoods. Lacking both the financial means to purchase expensive stereo systems and professional equipment and the knowledge of how to play musical instruments, these DJs used turntables and their record collections to become local performers. Splicing together songs from different albums representing a variety of musical genres (rock, disco, calypso, soul), they created patchwork compositions with danceable beats. A piece of a Led Zeppelin song might be joined with a piece of a Donna Summer song. Separate, the songs had nothing to do with one another. Played together through the complex working of two turntables and a mixer, a different song emerged. In essence, these DJs appropriated other songs and put them to new use. This act of appropriation offers us a lesson for cool writing. Instead of viewing hip-hop and DJs as only an object of study, we can learn ways to write from both these examples.

This process of joining pieces of different songs together to create a new song is called sampling. Today, sampling is done with computers called digital samplers, which can preserve bits of prerecorded music and save them for later usage. In the 1970s, however, sampling was done by locating specific grooves on a record that one wanted to hear and by mixing them with other moments on different records. In 1979, the band Sugar Hill Gang recorded the first major hip-hop hit with "Rapper's Delight." "Rapper's Delight" consisted of the music of Chic's disco hit "Freak Out" with new lyrics about teenage troubles. Although a live band recorded the song, "Rapper's Delight" introduced hip-hop's appropriative style to a mainstream audience.

Many of those who purchased "Rapper's Delight" in 1979 may have been unaware of the song's origins. The record didn't give credit to Chic for composing the music. The record company that produced "Rapper's Delight" didn't pay Chic royalties until Chic filed a lawsuit. Was Sugar Hill Gang obligated to do any of these things? Were they guilty of stealing Chic's song and profiting from the theft?

How is Sugar Hill Gang's usage of "Freak Out" a cool action? Does it fit with Baraka's definition? Does it matter that both Sugar Hill Gang and Chic were African-American bands? Baraka was only concerned with white appropriation of African-American music. What happens when this activity occurs within the same ethnic or racial group? Does a difference exist or not?

If you are not familiar with the song "Rapper's Delight" or any of the other songs mentioned in this chapter, go to this book's Web site for further information regarding how you can hear samples from the songs.

After the initial success of "Rapper's Delight," other groups quickly formed and found audiences for sampled compositions. Unlike Sugar Hill Gang, these groups tended to use either only sampled recordings or some combination of live band and samples. One of the most inventive of these artists was Grandmaster Flash. Rock band Blondie immortalized Grandmaster Flash in its hit "Rapture" with the line, "Flash is fast / Flash is cool." His 1981 *The Adventures of Grandmaster Flash on the Wheels of Steel* weaved an assortment of unrelated sounds such as old Flash Gordon serials, Blondie's "Rapture," The Temptations' "Can't Get Next To You," and other odds and ends to create a collage of music. In smooth transmission from one sample to the next, Grandmaster Flash redefines popular music and what we understand as "original" compositions. Is a collection of sampled material an original piece of work? Or is it merely a copy?

Do these questions ever arise in your own writing? For instance, in your writing classes, are you asked to "do your own work" or to turn in rough drafts along with final drafts in order to prove that you are the writer of the work you turn in? How would the composer of a sampled piece of songwriting do in a class that makes these demands? Would such a writer be accused of "cheating" or plagiarism? Why?

Sampling is not the first artistic practice to challenge our traditional conception of originals and copies. For example, in 1957, Pablo Picasso painted *Las Meninas*, a copy of the Spanish painter Velazquez's 1656 painting of the same name. Picasso's version copied the details of Velazquez's painting, yet the style was distinctly Picasso's. Was Picasso guilty of plagiarizing Velazquez's work? Or was he making an artistic statement about copies? Was this an homage to an influence or a theft? Search the Internet for examples of these two works. Are they really the same? How are they the same and how are they different?

There are other artists, songwriters, and poets who used past creations as the basis of their own work. Do some research on these movements and people, and see how they copied previous work and made it their own:

The Pop Art movement

Poet T. S. Eliot

Early Blues singers

1930s German photomontage artists

Russian filmmaker Sergei Eisenstein

Make a list of these movements and people. On one side, name the work that does the appropriating. On the other side of your list, indicate the work that was appropriated. Do these historical instances justify the practice of sampling in writing classrooms today?

As hip-hop grew in popularity, other bands like Public Enemy, De La Soul, and A Tribe Called Quest attracted considerable attention for the unique ways they sampled previously recorded sounds and music. For example, all of Public Enemy's first two albums, *It Takes A Nation of Millions to Hold Us Back* and *Fear of A Black Planet*, were comprised from a multitude of sounds strung together. Sampling James Brown, political speeches, 1960s jazz, even the "I" of Bob Marley's "I Shot the Sheriff," Public Enemy redefined the application of appropriation. Unlike Baraka's concern that appropriation undermines African-American power, Public Enemy worked to create a sense of power in the African-American community. Their songs dealt with controversial topics like drug abuse, misogyny, teenage pregnancy, and investment in African-American community building projects. By focusing on topics of concern to the African-American community, Public Enemy strived to initiate social change. They worked to rectify what they felt local and national government policy ignored. Their music critiqued current power structures and argued for a revolution in how Americans think about race.

Go online and do a search for Public Enemy's *It Takes A Nation of Millions to Hold Us Back.* Find an image of the album cover. Notice where band members Chuck D and Flavor Flav position themselves: in a prison cell. What kind of "cool" message are they trying to convey? How does the visual work in this image to convey a sense of coolness?

What groups like Public Enemy teach us, though, is that appropriation can function in empowering ways. What does it mean when a previously oppressed ethnic group suddenly finds itself capable of using the dominant groups' cultural productions for its own purposes? Unlike Elvis Presley's recording the work of black artists without properly compensating them, for instance, Public Enemy represents African-American usage of white music without financial compensation to the respected white artists.

From the Public Enemy example, we can generalize to ask a few questions relevant to how we rhetorically construct meaning in new media:

- Does a difference exist when one ethnic or racial group appropriates another? In which case(s)? Why?
- Is Public Enemy's appropriation of white performers (as opposed to the music industry's long history of whites appropriating African-American music) a case of two wrongs canceling each other out? Or do two wrongs never make a right?

- Should groups like Public Enemy be held accountable when white artists and production companies haven't been?
- Does Public Enemy's actions represent a form of protest as they often claim it does? What kind of protest is it, then? Should this type of protest be allowed, or should financial considerations limit one's ability to engage in dissent when it involves using work others have created?
- We saw in earlier chapters how cool's ties to economics play out in advertising and on the World Wide Web. Why shouldn't the same conditions apply to music? Don't musicians have the right to do what advertisers and Web designers do with cool?
- Public Enemy appropriates for purposes of critique. In early chapters, how did various Web sites appropriate cool?
- Spend some time listening to music by Public Enemy, The Beastie Boys, De La Soul, or any other hip-hop group that samples. On this book's Web site, you'll find links to these groups' music. Do you hear the distinctness of the samples? If so, how do you feel when you recognize the sample's origins? Do you see it as an act of theft? If you don't recognize the sample's origins, does it make a difference in your listening experience? Why?
- Return to our previous breakdown of Baraka's definition of cool. Does Public Enemy's sampling rhetorically match Baraka's cool?

Gettin' Jiggy Wit It

Other examples of appropriation in hip-hop include less politicized compositions. Since we don't want to overgeneralize and consider all hip-hop music as the same, we also need to look at the rhetorical value of appropriative gestures created strictly for commercial purposes. Unlike Public Enemy's approach to appropriation, these artists often take past compositions and rework them without much attention paid to the actual act of appropriation. Consequently, the borrowing of past styles seems innocuous and inconsequential. Will Smith's "Gettin' Jiggy Wit It" provides a good demonstration of this process. In 1997, "Gettin' Jiggy Wit It" sold several million copies, revitalized Will Smith's singing career, and was one of the year's most popular songs. Few of Smith's fans, however, may have known that "Gettin' Jiggy Wit It," like Sugar Hill Gang's remake of "Freak Out," is also the result of appropriation. "Gettin' Jiggy Wit It" appropriates the music of Sister Sledge's 1979 hit "He's The Greatest Dancer." Listeners who purchased Smith's album most likely remained unaware of this detail. A teenager who purchased the song in 1997 may not even have been born when Sister Sledge's single hit the charts. Go to the accompanying Web site for this book and find more information regarding the relationship between Sister Sledge's song and Will Smith's.

Smith's song also lacks the hard-edged quality of Public Enemy's politically oriented appropriations. While Public Enemy often speak of inner city life and the consequences of oppression, Smith's song speaks to an audience looking for new dance moves. With its commercially driven production, "Gettin' Jiggy Wit It" resembles any other cover version of a pop song. Another example is P-Diddy's (previously known as Puff Daddy, and before that, Sean Combs) 1997 "I'll Be Missing You," which samples The Police's "Every Breath You Take." P-Diddy's music, like Will Smith's, uses only one sample instead of a multitude of previous recordings. Thus, recognition of the song's origins becomes instantaneous and the complex interaction of different positions is absent.

Compare a song like P-Diddy's "I'll Be Missing You" with Public Enemy's "Fight the Power." What is the difference between the ways the two songs sample? What is the overall effect of these distinct sampling practices on you? How do you respond to the different sampling styles?

As we recognize how sampling creates varied responses, we begin to address the question of audience. When we write, we must always be aware of our audience. The recognition of one's audience is a rhetorical act. Who are we writing for? Who will read our work? All audiences are not the same. The way you write for your instructor differs from how you write a note to a member of your family or how you write a letter of application for a job. Public Enemy appears to write for an African-American audience; most of their songs deal with issues related to contemporary African-American experience. Similarly, their choice of samples relates to their expected audience. When Public Enemy, for example, samples James Brown, one reason they do so is because of James Brown's familiarity in the African-American community. Brown's iconic status makes him a recognizable figure. As we saw with Nike's usage of basketball star Jason Williams, iconic placement can initiate immediate recognition from an audience and thus prompt a desired response. Thus, we need to consider how sampling gives cool writers a tool for reaching audiences in new ways. When we draw upon isolated moments that will be familiar to our audiences, we grant our writing a persuasive advantage. Using recognizable and familiar material in our writing can be advantageous to making a specific point. At the end of this chapter, several of the writing exercises will ask you to practice sampling in different ways. Keep in mind the points raised in this section as you do so.

Is This Stealing?

As we examine hip-hop's treatment of appropriation, we need to keep in mind the conflicting relationships between appropriation and stealing. A fine line divides the two, and we may not discover a simple formula that helps differentiate between a moment of appropriation and a moment of theft (a point alluded to earlier in this chapter). In school, we define the latter activity as plagiarism. Plagiarism, schools often teach, involves the deliberate attempt to pass another's work off as one's own. If you turn in a paper that someone else wrote, you are guilty of plagiarism. But what happens when you appropriate another's work or a selection of another's work and make it your own, the way samplers do? Is this also plagiarism? Or is it a legitimate form of writing?

What we need is a way to differentiate between the two areas, to figure out where the gray areas are, and to ask how can we practice appropriation in our writing classes without being accused of plagiarism.

As a class, set some common guidelines identifying what plagiarism entails. Then do the same for sampling. What differentiates the two? Can you write new guidelines that find a common ground between the two and that will pertain to your writing class?

Think about how you are typically told to "Do your own work" in the classes you've taken or are taking now. If we compare this instructional directive with sampling's appropriative style, a number of questions arise:

- What is the difference between this instruction and the lesson hip-hop teaches us regarding writing?
- Is it possible to do "our own work" while the rhetorical act of appropriation maintains a constant presence in writing (whether we identify that presence or not)?
- Do any of our ideas just appear out of nowhere? Are our ideas only the result of our independent thinking? Or are we, in fact, always appropriating when we draw upon other sources for information or inspiration?

For instance, in addition to sampling other musical recordings, groups like Public Enemy also sample the sounds and people who influenced their attitudes. These sounds include both popular culture and political figures. Since Public Enemy maintains an interest in civil rights, their decision to sample a speech by Martin Luther King demonstrates King's influence on a particular position the group professes. Even King, however, sampled. Read King's canonical text "Letter from Birmingham Jail," which describes King's indignation with segregation (you can find additional information regarding this essay on this book's Web site). Arrested and imprisoned for protesting Alabama's discrimination policies, King composed this protest by drawing upon a variety of cultural references he knew would appeal to his audience. King's text is full of references to other works such as the Bible, philosophical texts, political writings and events, speeches, and even poetry. Can we consider King's writing to be an example of sampling as well? If so, do we accuse King of plagiarizing?

As we mentioned earlier regarding Public Enemy's usage of James Brown, King's sampling is also *audience* directed. For the samples to have a strong, rhetorical effect, an audience needs to be able to recognize the samples to some extent. When King begins "Letter from Birmingham Jail" with the biblical sampling of the Apostle Paul carrying the gospel throughout the Greco-Roman world, he does so in order to draw attention to the importance of the message he similarly is carrying to a Southern audience. The specific sample is meant to apply to a largely Christian, white audience who can identify easily with the reference because of the audience's familiarity with biblical tales. Consequently, the audience will draw a comparison between Paul's work and King's, and find King's cause sympathetic. When choosing what to sample, then, you need to be aware of what kind of audience you will present your work to and how your work will affect that audience.

Make a list comparing the differences or similarities between sampling and plagiarism. Try to come up with a definition, or series of definitions, that differentiates the two practices. You might also want to do some research on how the legal system understands sampling's relationship to intellectual property. Look up the case of the Turtles' lawsuit against De La Soul, which De La Soul lost. See how the courts ruled against sampling. How has that ruling affected sampling's ability to rhetorically construct new meanings? How should you include information like this ruling into your own definitions? Find more contemporary legal battles between those who sample and those who claim the practice as an infringement on their economic rights.

Further Listening

Public Enemy. *It Takes A Nation of Millions To Hold Us Back.* UNI/Def Jam, 1988.

Public Enemy. *Fear of A Black Planet.* Def Jam, 1990.

Beastie Boys. *Paul's Boutique.* Capitol Records, 1989.

De La Soul. *3 Feet High and Rising.* Tommy Boy, 1989.

A Tribe Called Quest. *The Low End Theory.* Jive, 1991.

Grandmaster Flash. *The Adventures of Grandmaster Flash on the Wheels of Steel.* Strut, 2002.

Further Reading

Amerika, Mark. "Avant-Pop Manifesto." Avant-Pop: The Stories of Mark Amerika. The 10th Special Exhibition, An Internet Art Retrospective Covering the Years 1993–2001.http://plaza.bunka.go.jp/bunka/museum/kikaku/exhibition10/english/ns/main2.html. Amerika's online writing fuses the appropriation strategies of hip-hop (what Amerika calls "playgiarism") with hypertextual writing.

George, Nelson. *Hip Hop America.* New York: Viking, 1998.

King, Martin Luther Jr. "Letter..." http://historicaltextarchive.com/sections/php?ap=viewarticle&artid=40.

Light, Alan, ed. *The Vibe History of Hip Hop.* New York: Three Rivers Press, 1999.

Rose, Tricia. *Black Noise: Black Music and Black Culture in Contemporary America.* Hanover: Wesleyan University Press, 1994.

Toop, David. *Rap Attack: African Jive to New York Hip Hop.* Boston: South End Press, 1984.

Web Site

On this book's Web site, examine some of the appropriated song examples provided. See how they compare with this chapter's examples. What other songs would you add? E-mail the author of this book with your suggestions.

Class Discussion

1. What are the economic consequences of appropriation? Can appropriation be a detriment to business? Why? Why not? How might it benefit business practices?

2. What are the political consequences of appropriation? How can it function as an act of empowerment? Consider how certain groups in your community feel shut out from the political system. How might they use appropriation to get their voices heard?

3. As a class, listen to some examples of sampled music. De La Soul, Public Enemy, or the Beastie Boys might make good choices. What samples do you recognize? What do the samples do in each song? Are they important to the song's content? If you removed the samples, would the meaning of the song change? How does your specific cultural position determine whether or not you are an appropriate audience for the compositions you hear? What kinds of audiences do these compositions appeal to?

Exercises: Appropriation and Sampling

1. Hip-hop's lesson on how to write cool involves appropriation. Appropriation is a rhetorical strategy that allows us to think about how to design cool sites. This writing exercise asks you to appropriate a Web site's code for your own purposes. This assignment also returns us to a similar exercise we did in Chapter 5. As you work through this exercise, return to the questions this chapter poses regarding appropriation and plagiarism.

   • Surf the Web for a page you like because of the way it looks. You might find sites with interesting overall designs or sites that require interactivity, for example. Web browsers come with a special feature that allows you to see how these pages are constructed. On Netscape, the feature is under View, and it is called "Page Source." On Internet Explorer, it is under View and called "Source." By choosing this option, you can see the HTML code used to create the page.

   • Look at the HTML code on the Web site you've chosen. Copy it and paste it into a new file on your HTML editing program. Then remove the content of the Web site, but keep the code mostly intact. (This is a tricky step that will require some trial and error. Don't get discouraged if you make mistakes and accidentally remove important code. If that happens, simply start over.)

- Replace the site's original content with your own.

- Link to your appropriated site a short essay outlining how you have either appropriated or plagiarized the site you borrowed from. What is your rationale? What is your evidence for one position or the other?

2. Go to one of the many JavaScript libraries available on the Web like JavaScript. com (http://www.javascript.com/) and JavaScript Source (http://javascript. internet.com/), or visit some of the DHTML (dynamic HTML) sites like Netscape's library (http://developer.netscape.com/docs/examples/dynhtml. html) or DHTML Central (http://www.dhtmlcentral.com/). You can also visit this book's Web site for further links. Experiment with copying some of the codes these sites offer. See how you can appropriate them for new purposes on your site.

3. Practice sampling. Collect a significant amount of images and quotations from recent newspapers and magazines. Your choices should be fairly current so that they will be recognizable to your audience (which we'll assume is your class). Then create a Web site that uses these "sampled" items you've gathered to support a position you have on a current issue. Some issues you might write about could include: the environment, a regional conflict, local or national politics, a sports event, etc.

   In other words, just as hip-hop uses samples to reach its audience, use the samples to create your writing and insights for your own audience. Work with hyperlinks and images to create your sampled site.

4. Perform the same assignment but focus your topic on a current community problem in your area. Construct a sampled Web site that responds to this problem by sampling newspaper articles, magazine stories, advertisements, political statements, interviews, e-mail discussion, etc. so that the end result forms a critique or alternative perspective on the problem. Choose from a wide variety of different kinds of material.

   Your audience for this assignment is the party responsible for the problem or for fixing the problem. When you are through, e-mail the party responsible for the problem with the address of your Web site and ask them for a response to the writing you have created.

Chapter

8

Manhood

A considerable amount of writing about cool concentrates on the question of manhood and masculinity. In this chapter, we'll look at several approaches to the male figure. In mass media representations (and often in daily discourse), cool figures tend to be described or imagined as males, sometimes muscular, who stand in aloof poses, dress fashionably, and are often physically attractive. As we'll see throughout this chapter, commentary on cool often ignores female participation and instead turns cool into a male-dominated phenomenon. In the past, traditional male figures who embrace the persona of cool have included James Dean, Marlon Brando, and Elvis Presley. These male figures play a dominant role in American popular culture. In movies they represent the misunderstood hero; his "badness" makes the audience suspect him and not trust him, but deep down he's the good guy, the one we root for.

In Chapter 3, we saw how advertising plays off this representation, and in particular, how Web hosting company .TV appropriates James Dean's image to sell its services. We may have never seen a James Dean film, but we immediately recognize Dean as cool, and in turn the company that utilizes his image must be cool, too. Other examples can be found in Marlon Brando's depiction of a motorcycle gang leader in the 1957 film *The Wild One*, an image appropriated by various TV shows, comic strips, and advertisements as well. Wearing a leather jacket and acting as the leader of a gang, Brando's character Johnny exudes the stereotypical cool attributes of toughness and rebellion. Think about films popular today. What characters appear tough on the screen and appear as antagonists, but simultaneously represent the hero?

While these examples are all white actors, what about African-American male figures? How do they fit into the cool stereotype? Media representations of African-American male figures include film roles (played by actors like Denzel Washington), television characters (like those created by Bill Cosby), sports figures (Michael Jordan) and political figures (former Atlanta mayor Andrew Young or Secretary of State Colin Powell). While these figures capture different images of the black male, they don't necessarily reflect the cool male. In popular media, the cool black male possesses similar traits to the typical white figure, with added elements that specifically reflect African-American experience.

- Besides James Dean or Marlon Brando, what other white popular culture figures do we typically label as cool?
- Which black males do we consider cool?
- Are there differences between the two sets of males? Or do both sets maintain the same characteristics?
- Is the comparison of black and white males a problematic practice? Is there something wrong with doing this kind of comparison or do we accept it as a normal method for differentiating between male representations?
- What about females? Why is cool often restricted to males? How can we supplement this discussion with female examples?

Picking up from the previous chapter's discussion of hip-hop, we can begin a discussion of black masculinity by looking at music. In hip-hop, when we think of African-American celebrities who have adopted the word cool into their names—rap stars like L.L. Cool J, Kool Moe D, Coolio, Kool Keith, and DJ Kool—they are almost always male. Watching their videos, we see these stars as advertisements for cool masculinity. Often bare-chested, wearing fashionable clothing and jewelry, posing for the camera in seductive yet threatening ways, these figures are almost caricatures of how males behave. They resemble Charles Schultz' Snoopy, from his comic strip *Peanuts*. From time to time, Snoopy dresses up as "Joe Cool," a college undergraduate who "hangs out" on campus, wears dark sunglasses, and tries to "pick up" girls. To be cool, these male figures seem to state, is to be consistently on the lookout for sexual adventure. Thus, in their performances, these types of hip-hop artists indicate that gender and cool have a distinct relationship.

Hip-hop's role in the larger entertainment culture includes shaping expectations about how genders behave and are perceived publicly. When we ask who have been some of entertainment's most imposing figures, for instance, the answer usually is the same: men. Scanning the weekly entertainment magazines, we see the familiar images of males like Tom Cruise and Russell Crowe. While not only males exemplify cool, we need to examine why and how various media forms explore cool as a masculine characteristic. At the same time, we need to ask why females are often excluded from these definitions of cool and how we can rectify this absence. In this chapter, we will explore these questions. Consequently, we'll see that a gendered position regarding cool proliferates in popular culture. This position tends to dominate how we read cool across gendered lines and even leads to a variety of cultural biases.

> Do an online search for images of hip-hop performers like Nas or L.L. Cool J. Notice how they often pose: arms crossed, tough look. How is the rhetoric of this pose masculine and not feminine? Why does it matter if we describe the pose as gendered?

The White Negro

In 1957, cultural critic Norman Mailer wrote the provocative essay "The White Negro." Mailer's essay attempted to describe the American response to the devastation of World War II, the dropping of the atomic bomb on the Japanese cities of Hiroshima and Nagasaki, and the Holocaust. Horrified by these experiences, Americans, Mailer felt, needed to turn their attention to something that would alleviate the trauma of the previous decade. For Mailer, African-American culture contained the solution. Unsettled white males, confused and perplexed over what to do with their lives, traumatized by the war, needed an alternative lifestyle. White males admired the supposed sexuality of African-American males, Mailer contended, and used African-American behavior as the basis for excitement and thrills. These white males, who Mailer named the "White Negroes," copied the behavior, dress, and language of African-American males in an effort to be cool. To be cool, Mailer claimed, was to exemplify the African-American experience, which he felt was a "primitive" sexual experience always in search of the perfect "orgasm," an animal-like experience that only cared about pleasure and ignored intellectual pursuits.

Mailer's view of African-American masculinity remains a cornerstone for how cool can inspire racism. Labeling a culture as "sexual" or "primitive" casts a painful stereotype over an entire group of people. And to refer specifically to African-American culture as exemplifying these traits taps into white America's worst perceptions of African-Americans as "jungle people" or "primitives." While Mailer's essay is almost fifty years old, its effect on contemporary thinking cannot be ignored. When we speak about cool and masculinity, we must remember where certain stereotypes come from, how they've been written about, and how little may have changed since their inception. Mailer's distorted understanding of the African-American male is still prevalent today. On this book's Web site, you can find short excerpts from Mailer's essay and further information regarding its influence.

Even though Mailer's essay is almost fifty years old and is racist in its origins, we can reapply its thinking. Do white males still attempt to imitate other racial and ethnic groups? Can you think of contemporary popular culture figures we might call "white Negroes," not because they embody sexuality, but because they represent the racial blurring of black and white cultures?

Does there exist a current term that describes white males who act African-American? What about white females who act African-American? What do you think about how such words are used? Is this a fair description? If not, for whom is it not fair?

What are the rhetorical effects of these kinds of racial labels?

Journalist and commentator Donnell Alexander indirectly takes up Mailer's confusion of black masculinity with uncontrolled sexuality in his 1997 essay "Are Black People Cooler Than White People?" Beginning with an anecdote about the male, black experience, Alexander quickly points out how stereotypes proliferate easily in American culture. Alexander's neighbor, a new immigrant, looks suspiciously upon him whenever he arrives home to his apartment building. What, Alexander asks, does the neighbor fear? What does his color have to do with her overall perception of African-American males? Does she think he doesn't live in the building? Does she suspect him of wrongdoing? If so, why has she developed a fear of black males? Responding to his neighbor's fears, Alexander questions how television shows like *Cops* represent black males: shirtless, on drugs, and as criminals. Television, he claims, has created a "cool" male through the visual display (which we might call visual "writing") of someone who is too cool for society and must be imprisoned for regular transgression of the law. The woman, Alexander believes, lives in a "cool world" because her preconditioned assumptions and fears instruct her to associate all black males with a stereotype perpetuated by the dominant culture.

Stereotypes are rhetorical; they develop from the various representations we read, see, and create. A stereotype, therefore, is culturally formed. While we don't have space to outline the various negative stereotypes associated with black males (or with any other group), we can address the role cool plays in both perpetuating such biases and countering them. And keeping with the spirit of resistance we encountered in Chapter 5, we can examine how the African-American community often counters such representations with its own versions of how a black male should be viewed. These responses will teach us specific strategies we can use in our own writing.

There remains, however, a danger in our own analysis and exploration of black masculinity. We, too, might generalize and stereotype through our efforts to define the black, cool male. We must keep in mind, therefore, that this discussion does not reflect a representation of actual black males, but rather how the *idea* of the "black male" has been represented as cool in certain media forms. In other words, our discussion differentiates from actual people and the images such people portray. We are discussing the images, not the people.

Fight the Power

One dominant image of African-American masculinity involves the always-fighting male figure, the so-called "angry black man." Encouraged by its appearance in films, on television, and in musical representations, "angry black man" has become a common stereotype to describe black males who disagree with mainstream culture, express anger at injustice, or who look for alternative means of expression. Critics of MTV's soap opera *The Real World*, for example, often point to the persistent role of an angry black man (Kevin from *Real World 1*, David from *Real World 9*) among the cast's other characters, season after season. Films of the 1970s often perpetuated the image of the angry black man through such representations as Shaft, played by Richard Roundtree, or Superfly, played by Ron O'Neal. Typically, a resident of the inner city or a broken home, the angry black man represents the disenfranchised individual denied any means to enter the social or political system. In 1999, Aaron McGruder introduced his now popular comic strip *The Boondocks* by representing the strip's main character, Huey Freeman, as a prototypical angry young black man. In an April 19, 1999 strip, Huey tells his brother Riley that their move from Chicago to the suburbs is far from "the hard streets of the south side."

> "Do you understand what I'm trying to say," Huey asks his brother.
> "I think so," his brother responds. "I'm the hardest, baddest thing for miles and I can run amok here without fear."

Click on http://www.thenation.com/cover.mhtml?i=20020128 and you can see the cover portrait *The Nation* magazine devoted to this representation of the angry young black man. Another *Boondocks* strip, located online at http://images.ucomics.com/images/uclick/boondocks.gif, shows Huey trying to get a revolutionary manifesto of his ideas syndicated in nationwide newspapers. Huey's friend Caesar responds to the effort by asking whether or not millions of Americans are "ready to wake up to the rantings of an angry black kid." These examples demonstrate how a comic strip like *The Boondocks* attempts to use humor in order to break down racial stereotypes like the angry black man.

Locate online other representations of angry black men and discuss how these images make you feel. What specific attributes do the writers of these representations make? In other words, are these figures dressed a certain way, located in specific areas, or situated in specific poses?

Are there parallel images and stereotypes for women? If not, what other stereotypes might prevent women from being labeled "angry"? In other words, how does our culture "write" the image of women so that they are not angry?

In music, the African-American record label Death Row provides an example of how violence and anger can be used for entertainment purposes so that "the angry black man" becomes an empty sign of black masculinity. In other words, the social or political reasons for anger are removed and are rhetorically replaced by cultural markers of anger (dress, attitude, style) that fail to reflect the issue's origins. Innovators of the "gangsta" image within hip-hop, a style of rap originating in south central Los Angeles and the Compton neighborhood, Death Row established a violent version of cool in this vein: the detached and distant African-American male seeking vengeance on society for all of its past wrongdoings. Gangsta rap, as this form of hip-hop is called, involves the fierce imagery and attitudes often associated with street life. In addition to borrowing the word "gangster" from 1930s and 1940s films and culture, gangsta rap also appropriates a considerable amount of traditional gangster themes, most associated with the gangster image in popular culture. Some typical characteristics of the gangsta include:

- Outlaw image
- Open violence in lyrics and lifestyle
- Misogyny
- Disdain for mainstream society

Nicknamed G-Funk, gangsta rap includes such performers as Ghostface Killah (Tony Starks), N.W.A. (Niggaz With Attitude), and Ice Cube (O'Shea Jackson). Their music appropriated 1970s funk and applied new themes of street life, disrespect for women, and gang-related behavior. Many of these artists also used their music to attack other gangsta rappers who recorded for different labels.

During its heyday, Death Row records, run by Suge Knight, produced a significant amount of gangsta rap. Death Row's artists borrowed heavily from the traditional "bad boy" image often associated with cool males, an image typically aligned with James Dean or Marlon Brando. These artists, Dr. Dre (Andre Young), Snoop Doggy Dogg (Calvin Broadus), and Tupac Shakur (Lesane Crooks), acted like gang members, calling themselves by the moniker "thug." Their songs spoke of rivalries and fighting, abuse and violence, breaking the law and serving prison time. Like the films *Boyz in the The Hood*, *Colors*, *New Jack City*, or *Menace II Society*, these rappers draw attention to the brutal life of the inner city. In the end, however, the boundaries between describing the inner city and becoming celebrities blurred. The purpose of all of their work was to make money and provide musical enjoyment to listeners. Death Row Records, after all, functioned as a business.

Death Row propagated the image of the male as "thug." Are there corresponding images of women as "thugs" as well? Where? Which record labels? Which Web sites? Which films or TV shows?

Death Row is a good example of how the line between reality and image became distorted as musical artists grow more successful. At some point, the image of toughness that was meant to draw attention to street life transformed simultaneously into caricature and real-life experience. While many of the gangsta images produced by labels like Death Row seem cartoonish, some of the musicians began to take their gangsta image too seriously, imagining themselves as real life outlaws and not popular culture figures. Consequently, the violence they sung about eventually turned real as several members met untimely deaths.

The example of Death Row prompts the question: at what point does popular mythology overtake reality? At one point do we start believing in myths (like that of the rebel or outlaw) and stop believing in the world around us? Or to put the question another way: at what point do myths constitute the basis for reality? Myths are stories we create to make sense of the world. You might be familiar with Greek or Roman mythology, for instance, which helped Greek and Roman cultures explain the origins of the world. The Native American trickster figure marks another mythological creation used by various Native American tribes to help explain where certain items came from or why we behave in confusing ways.

In contemporary culture, if one is from an impoverished neighborhood, sees no chance to rise above poverty and crime, and feels that mainstream culture won't allow any chance for self-improvement because of one's race, then creating a myth of empowerment (like the gangsta image) can help make sense of a hopeless situation. The gangsta image, therefore, allows one a chance to write a new image for oneself. The French literary critic Roland Barthes states, "myth gives a natural image" of reality. Barthes suggests that we form myths in order to construct a version of reality we will be most comfortable with. Following Barthes' observation, we can consider cool's relationship to the gangster image as one of mythology. The gangsta image allows oppressed groups of people a degree of comfort because it provides the image of fighting back against the system.

> Consider how cool might function as myth. How is it used to make sense of the world?
>
> Make a list of all of the things we've discussed so far related to cool. Which of these meet our criteria for what a myth entails? What else would you add?
>
> Would you say that this book "mythologizes" cool even further? Why or why not?

The flip side of the myth of the gangsta is that gangstas can only be men. Or to put it slightly differently, the gangsta attitude can only be adopted by men. Is this true? Typically, the gangsta attitude degrades women, treating them as uncool. Female rappers who adopt tough personalities, like Lil Kim, Queen Latifah, Da Brat, and Foxy Brown, would probably disagree with this notion. If anything, we might too eagerly attribute the gangsta role to men because such a move offers us some level of comfort (we feel better thinking men are powerful and women aren't). Our job as writers and critics, though, is to redirect such myths. Why do men find it more comfortable to imagine themselves as "tough guys"? Why do many men find tough women to be threatening? Does each image carry specific rhetorical meanings?

To understand the mythical effect of gangsta rap on popular thought, we also need to understand some of the personalities, as well as the images they created, that form the medium. Doing so will help us break down the gangsta's rhetoric and think about what we can learn for our own writing. Research the images portrayed by these hip-hop figures:

- Tupac Shakur—Killed by unknown gunmen in 1996, Shakur's image has since taken on mythical status.
- Biggie Smalls (Notorious B.I.G.)—One-time friend, then enemy, of Tupac, Biggie Smalls was also gunned down.
- Suge Knight—Founder and head of Death Row Records. Knight took on the role of mob boss regarding the artists he signed. Eventually, he was sent to prison.

> These are male descriptions. What female rappers would you add to this list and what types of mythic personalities do they portray? For example, look up online the lyrics to Missy Elliott's "Work It." What is she singing about? Is she assuming power in sexual relationships? Does that make her a gangsta, too?

After you have gathered some background information on these figures, imagine them as constructing mythical personas. Do these personas match any other mythical figures you've read about on your own or in other classes? Then look over the following excerpts from their music. Think about how these song lyrics from Death Row artists reflect the image of cool as anger.

ALL EYES ON ME

Until I die Live the life of a Boss playa, cuz even when I'm high
f**k with me and get crossed later, the futures in my eyez
Cuz all I want is cash and thangs,
A five double 0 Benz and flaunting flashy rings

> *Tupac Shakur*

THE DOGGFATHER

I put down more hits than mafioso made
And Lucky Lucianno 'bout to sing soprano
And I know, I know the way you feel
And baby bubba we gon' keep it on tha real
Just to get you caught up in amazement
We puffin' on Cubans so it might get dangerous
But when it isn't, you can sit izzon bizzack
And let the Bizzow Wizzow ride the trizzack, ha ha
How you feelin'? I'm up to dealin', ridin' like a villain

> *Snoop Dogg*

LET IT RIDE

Creepin' down the back street on Deez.
I got my glock cocked 'cause niggaz want these.
Now, soon as I said it,
Seems I got sweated
By some nigga with a tech-9
Tryin' to take mine.
You wanna make noise, make noise.
I make a phone call my niggaz comin' like the Gotti boys.
Bodies bein' found on Greenleaf
With their f**kin heads cut off.

> *Dr. Dre*

How do these lyrics reflect the "bad boy" image prevalent in cool masculinity? What kind of imagery do they use? What kind of language? What parts of their language do you find difficult to decipher? Why? Do the lyrics distort words? Do these lyrics assume that listeners will immediately understand the meanings? What kind of audience, then, do these rappers assume will buy their music? Do these lyrics emphasize money or consumer goods? How? All of these questions can lead us to a better understanding regarding the rhetorical construction of the gangsta image.

The objects we buy are called commodities. Take these excerpts as rationale to further explore gangsta lyrics. How often are commodity names inserted in the lyrics? Here we see Mercedes Benz, Cuban cigars, and Glock pistols. What else is mentioned in these and other songs? What is the relationship between commodities and the song's content? How do commodities guide the songs' movement from idea to idea? Why do you think gangsta lyrics appear obsessed with owning expensive goods?

Lyrics are a form of writing, even if this is not the type of writing you are typically asked to do in school. We can still, however, learn from these lyrics various ways to borrow ideas from popular culture. If you were to write a short statement about an issue important to you (for instance, a tense global situation, a local problem at your university or college, a community problem), what kinds of commodity names would you draw upon for examples and evidence to support your argument? The lyrics we just examined use Mercedes Benz and Cuban cigars as representative of some statement regarding toughness. What items can you choose which will be relevant to your audience and make clear to them your point? If you were writing your argument for the Web, how would you use images of these items to support your claim? (Think back to the chapter on icons.)

We also need to ask how these artists contrast sharply with the hip-hop performers we've examined previously. How can we explain the discrepancies in how each group fits with cool? Public Enemy, for example, is about a cool style, appropriation, as writing. Death Row Records, on the other hand, is about using songwriting to create the cool, rebellious personality. Nevertheless, each case still uses writing, albeit it is writing in different ways. We can generalize from these songwriting examples in order to apply their lessons to our own writing (as the previous paragraph asks you to do).

An additional lesson tells us that just as it is important to cool writing to understand personality, it is equally important to understand a medium's language. Research these common terms found in gangsta rap's language:

- Thug
- Homeboy
- G-thing
- Fronting
- Keeping it real
- Represent
- Phat
- Getting schooled
- Trippin'

How are these terms used rhetorically? In other words, how are they used to create meaning in given situations? What other media have developed their own language and mythologies? Sports? News broadcasting? School? Instead of calling a class "phat" at your school, what word might your teachers or administrators use?

Another excellent example of language and hip-hop (though not a gangsta examples) comes from Missy Elliott's popular song "Work It." In this song, Missy Elliott challenges our expectations of language by recording the chorus backwards. Elsewhere in the song, she tries to imitate sounds associated with sexual activity. In one stanza, Missy Elliott sings:

> "Love the way my ass go ba-bomp-a-bomp-bomp Keep your eyes on my ba-bomp-a-bomp-bomp You think you can handle this ka-donk-a-donk-donk? Take my thong off and my ass go BOOM! Cut the lights on so you can see what I can do."

Even though you may find the lyrics a bit sensational for your class, think about how she uses language not typical to everyday conversation in order to make a point about dancing and sexuality. What do you make of the repetitive phrasing? The exclamations? How could you apply her style to a Web site you are creating?

On this book's Web site, you can find more information about this song and its lyrics, as well as ways to use it as a model for Web writing.

Do you consider yourself a participant in any specific form of expression (in sports, school, music, etc.) or an observer? As we observe gangsta culture here, we might feel more like outsiders looking in than as participants in the gangsta experience. But what happens when you apply the notions of language construction and mythology to a culture you belong to, like school? Can you make a list of terms specific to other discourses? How do we eventually become acquainted with specialized language? What is the rhetorical value of developing and maintaining a specialized language, whether that language uses a term like "tripping" or something else?

Much of the work done by Public Enemy and the attitudes appropriated by gangsta rap stem from the Black Panthers' influence. Led by Eldridge Cleaver and Huey Newton, the Black Panthers introduced the notion of black militancy to late 1960s and early 1970s American culture.

Frustrated with what they felt was complacency within the civil rights movement, the Black Panthers opted for a military solution to the problem of inequality. The rest of American culture interpreted their efforts, however, not as a cause for social justice, but rather an encouragement for violence. White America understood the Panther rhetoric of "revolution" as not a plea for equality but violent attacks on white culture. Therefore, while contributing to the cause of civil rights, they also helped perpetuate the stereotype of the "angry black man."

Ali and Media Representation

Another place where the angry black man image appears is in sports. In sports, the example of boxing legend Muhammad Ali demonstrates how the angry black man stereotype works. Like Ali, black males are often depicted as engaged in a persistent battle with overpowering forces: discrimination, unemployment, and inferior housing conditions comprise some of these problems. Ali's forces, of course, were opponents in the ring. Ali, though, marks the real life representation of the angry man as more than just a shallow, brooding figure displayed on television, in film, or in music. Unlike Death Row records, Ali developed more than an image; he worked towards rectifying real-life social inequality through specific rhetorical acts. Ali made his mark not only as a world champion boxer who fought opponents in the ring, but as a fighter for social justice.

In 1964, Ali converted to Islam and changed his name from Cassius Clay. For Ali, the act signified a rhetorical protest against white policies towards African-Americans. Ali felt that if a white government refused to recognize him as equal, he didn't want a white name. The move also mirrored Malcolm X's refusal to go by his white name (Little). The X Malcolm X adopted as his surname symbolized white erasure of his African heritage. In addition, Ali's refusal in 1967 to serve in the military after being drafted caused turmoil in the sports and political spheres, who interpreted his gesture as an assault on American values and not as social protest. The New York Boxing Commission stripped Ali of his boxing license and revoked his championship. The government sentenced him to five years in prison for draft evasion. Ali's fight as a boxer extended to a fight with the government and the rest of the culture that judged him.

To position himself politically, Ali sought to form his own sense of self-definition. Society defined him as Cassius Clay. He changed his name to Muhammad Ali. When Ali declared "I'm the Greatest," we can imagine him speaking for all African-Americans who struggle to define themselves in spite of discrimination. Ali's remark is a form of self-identification. Much in the way Death Row artists identified themselves as "thugs" and "gangstas," Ali defined himself as "the greatest." The lesson for cool writing, then, involves self-identification. If the culture remains unable to see greatness in portions of its populace, for instance, then these people should define themselves as great. Ali's version of cool teaches us that power comes from the images we create for ourselves, not from images created for us by outside entities. We can better examine Ali's importance to cool by looking at the specific language he uses to identify himself. Think about these other Ali quotes:

- "I have wrestled with an alligator, I've tussled with a whale. I done unhandcuffed lightning, thrown thunder in jail. Only last week murdered a rock, injured a stone, hospitalized a brick. I'm so mean I make medicine sick."
- "Float like a butterfly, sting like a bee, I am the Greatest, Muhammad Ali."
- "I'm so fast I can turn out the light and be in bed before it's dark."
- "I was determined to be the nigger the white man didn't get."

Each of these statements, humorous or serious, marks an effort to define himself, or to write himself in a new public manner. In what ways does Ali define himself? How does he use language to do so? Why is self-definition an important cool trait? Does self-definition function as a resistance strategy? In other words, can it be used to resist overpowering and unjust discourses (like the right to name yourself)? How else does self-definition work as a cool act? When you identify yourself (i.e., when you make your name known to others), what steps do you take in order to make clear who you are and what you are about?

Changing your name has significant rhetorical meaning. It allows you to redefine yourself for a respective audience and to make a specific point while doing so. Ali changed his name to protest American racism. Malcolm X made a similar move, changing his name from what he felt was the racist "Little" to the more symbolic "X."

In hip-hop, name changes deal either with politics or with other kinds of cultural responses. Consider these name changes:

50 Cent

Eminem

Da Brat

Busta Rhymes

What kind of meanings do these names convey? Are the meanings economic? Cultural? Attitude-based? Research these figures and find out why they chose these names.

At the end of this chapter there is an exercise that asks you to think about the rhetorical act of changing your own name.

The continuing debate surrounding Ali's name change or refusal to fight in Vietnam questions the right of the black male (or any person of color) to define himself and not be defined by the rest of the culture. Ali's acts have specific historical origins. We can understand cool as self-definition slightly better when we examine the ways black culture has been represented on television and in film. These two media forms provide examples of how groups become socially defined by others. We can generalize from the examples to the work we do for the Web.

Historically, media definitions of the black male have not been flattering. Film and television often portray the black male figure as passive: a servant, a slave, or a so-called coon. Early television programs like *Amos 'N' Andy* and later shows like *Good Times* portrayed black males as bumbling or incompetent, symbolic for how many African-American experiences are depicted. *Good Times*, for instance, presented the image of an inner city African-American family dealing with the struggle to exist when opportunities are scarce. The seriousness of their travails, however, is minimized by the ways the show is framed. Consider the lyrics to the *Good Times* theme song:

Temporary layoff—Good Times!
Easy credit rip-off—Good Times!
Ain't we lucky we got 'em—Good Times!

The song appears to romanticize the urban black experience by stating that having no work or being economically taken advantage of equals good times. "Good Times" appears to mock the inner city experience as trivial.

We can understand these shows as part of an entertainment legacy of late nineteenth- and early twentieth-century minstrel shows in which white actors wore blackface and mocked African-American culture. In the minstrel show, actors performed as "authentic" black creations. In fact, the opposite was true. The minstrel show appropriated black culture as a means to denigrate black experience. Through song and dance, actors parodied African-American culture as inferior. Cultural markers of African-American culture, that is, the items which we use to identify each other, became recontextualized in racist ways. Dark skin was made to be even darker. Songs originating during slavery to express the hardships of oppression were turned into jokes.

This practice carried over into early cinema. The first movie to feature sound, *The Jazz Singer*, dealt with a man who wore blackface. And even when white actors weren't wearing blackface to mock African-American culture, Hollywood often made African-American entertainers behave as if they were minstrels. For example, one of the first black film stars was Steppin Fetchit, who played the stereotype of a lazy, unintelligent black male, a clown who mumbled phrases and scratched his head in a dumbfounded manner when perplexed by even the simplest task. Fetchit replied to others by saying "Yassuh" and "Nassuh," a clear indication that his position was meant to be inferior to his white counterparts.

Does the minstrel show remind you of something else we've discussed? Is the minstrel show a form of appropriation? Use the Internet to find images and posters of old minstrel shows.

Ask yourself what is being appropriated in these images.

Would you say that the gangsta image resembles the minstrel?

Another question to ask is if this is another form of cool representation? If so, how? If not, why is it different? Naming all cool representations as appropriation means we will find troubling practices, like the minstrel show, as indicative of cool. Our understanding of cool, then, must change accordingly.

In his film *Bamboozled*, director Spike Lee critiques entertainment culture's proliferation of such minstrel inspired images. Lee creates a fictitious TV show called *Mantan: The New Millennium Minstrel Show*, which features modern black actors wearing blackface. The message of Lee's critique is that traditional discriminatory practices still exist in contemporary entertainment culture. The ways we appropriate other cultures can quickly transform into racist practices. For Lee, black males have let their own images be appropriated by commercial culture. Consequently, they've lost control over how to represent themselves and have allowed the black male to be treated as just another blackface production.

In addition to the example of critique Lee presents, he also offers cool writing another lesson about form. Form is important to rhetoric. Form allows us to reach specific audiences in specific ways. By creating *a movie* about racism, Lee takes a medium often employed to spread racism (film) and creates a critique. As we saw with Adbusters' choice of form, Lee chooses a form other than the essay to establish critique. There exists a long tradition in film of demonizing or diminishing African-American culture, a tradition that includes D.W. Griffith's *Birth of a Nation* as well as *Gone With the Wind*. By working with film, Lee demonstrates how the tool of discrimination becomes a tool of resistance. We'll see this type of writing later when we examine cool in literature. Rather than write an article denouncing minstrel practices and their continued effect on popular culture, Lee uses film to express his views. His choice of medium doesn't negate the power of the essay, but it does offer an alternative form for critique. In this sense, Lee takes a dominant form of discourse and uses it as a platform for minority response.

The minstrel show features a cool male acquiescing to more powering cultural forces. But if we classify figures like Ali as cool as well, then we propose that another version of cool exists, one which is active and not passive. Social response becomes a cool trait. Under these terms, one can fight stereotypes by turning them around. Since, for instance, Ali was classified as an "angry black man" because of his race and age, he opted to demonstrate just how "angry" he was. He fought against laws that discriminated on the basis of skin color. In *Bamboozled*, racist television programming and film production eventually are redirected against those who perpetrated it in the first place. Regarding black masculinity, then, we have two versions of cool: passive and active cultural participant.

We now can think of all of these issues as ways the culture writes about its members. The songs, television shows, and movies are all forms of writing. The ways writers work in these media reflect active and passive strategies. These media raise important questions regarding how we write about ourselves.

- How often do you feel like you are actively engaging with writing? Do you ever feel that assignments don't allow you room to express your ideas in alternative forms? Which kinds of assignments? Why not? Do you feel that writing is a passive or active activity? How can it be both?
- How do you feel that the group you identify with is written about? Do you feel stereotyped at times? Why? Where do you see such stereotypes? On TV? In films? In advertisements?
- How do you represent yourself to others? If you feel stereotyped, how do you work around these initial perceptions you encounter? If you could "write yourself," how would you do it?
- Ali and Lee discussed male black images. Identify several female images that function in stereotypical ways. How easily do we accept these images as "real" or acceptable? What do we do to prevent such images from being accepted?
- Where is the proper place to write about ourselves and cultural roles? Ali chose the ring. Spike Lee chose film. What medium do you choose?

Further Reading

Alexander, Donnell. "Are Black People Cooler than White People?" *Might.* July-August, 1997.

Chipman, Dawn, Mari Florence, Naomi Wax, and Pam Nelson, eds. *Cool Women.* New York: 17th Street Press, 2001.

Coolwomen.org: http://www.coolwomen.org

Haley, Alex. *The Autobiography of Malcolm X.* New York, Ballantine Books, 1990.

Mailer, Norman. "The White Negro." *Advertisements for Myself.* Great Britain: Panther, 1968.

Marshall, Gary. "Murder as the Case." *Spike* Magazine. http://www.spike magazine.com/0300deathrow.htm. An analysis of Tupac Shakur's image.

Neal, Mark Anthony. *Soul Babies.* New York: Routledge, 2002.

Remnick, David. *King of the World: Muhammad Ali and the Rise of an American Hero.* New York: Random House, 1998.

Further Listening

Dr. Dre. *The Chronic.* Death Row, 2001.

The Notorious B.I.G. *Ready to Die.* Bad Boy, 1994.

Snoop Doggy Dogg. *Doggystyle.* Priority Records, 1993.

Tupac Shakur. *Thug Life.* Jive, 1995.

Further Viewing

When We Were Kings. Dir. Leon Gast. Polygram Video, 1996.

Bamboozled. Dir. Spike Lee. New Line Cinema, 2000.

Birth of a Nation. Dir. D. W. Griffith. Allied Artists Classic Library, 1915.

Web Site

On *Writing About Cool's* Web site, you'll find more information regarding hip-hop language. Visit the site for additional exercises regarding how to use only hip-hop language in order to write an essay for a class.

Class Discussion

1. Black males are often depicted as either engaging in sexual activity or fighting. Can you think of other stereotypes that proliferate in our culture regarding other gender and ethnic groups? Where do you find such stereotypes?

2. How do you feel students in your university or college are stereotyped? Why have these stereotypes proliferated? How do such stereotypes rhetorically function? In other words, how do they contribute to the ways we make meaning?

3. What happens when someone steps out of culturally preconceived roles? How do we typically respond? What happens when we apply race to the gendered role? Do we think of black men as different than white men? When

we examine these roles more carefully, where do we see exception? Do we, in fact, ever see many examples of the stereotype? Or is it an isolated issue?

4. Can we find female equivalents of Ali? Can we find equally demeaning female representations in films and on television as we've seen with the minstrel show?

5. Even though this chapter discusses females and cool to some extent, does it do a good enough job? Discuss which females you feel are missing from this chapter. Go to *Writing About Cool's* Web site and e-mail this book's author with names you feel should be covered in this chapter but aren't.

Exercises

1. Much of what we've discussed in this chapter deals with how a racial stereotype is formed and how the group stereotyped either adopts the image or resists it. For this assignment, we want to see if other groups experience similar situations.

    Choose an ethnic group. Using the Web, find as many ways (textually and visually) this ethnic group is represented. Save the images you discover. Write down where these discoveries come from so that you can cite their origins later. Look at magazines, advertisements, Usenet groups, celebrity fan sites, and newspapers.

2. Create a Web site in which you display your findings. Use rollovers, pop-ups, hyperlinks, and other scripts you can find in online script libraries. When you arrange the various images and citations, what kind of representation emerges? Then write a short essay describing your reaction to this representation. Is it an accurate depiction? Why or why not? How often are similar images and words used to describe this group? Do you find mostly female or male images? Do you see specific roles attributed to these groups?

3. Finally, juxtapose your essay into your Web site so that your observations merge with the visual findings you've presented. Your commentary, therefore, should be visually aligned with your images.

4. Both Spike Lee and Muhammad Ali provide examples of how we can resist negative writing about race. On a Web site, create a newsletter, pseudo-newspaper page, or advertisement that resists a negative, racial position. The position may include politics, international relations, school issues, or some other item. For reference, think about the previous examples of cool in advertising we've discussed.

5. Take Lee's project one step further. Remember, Lee uses film to critique racist practices in film. Create a Web site that critiques the politics of another Web site for its racial depictions.

6. *The Autobiography of* _____. Cool figures like Muhammad Ali teach a rhetorical lesson about the power of changing one's name. As mentioned earlier in this chapter, name changes are popular in hip-hop culture in which rappers take on new names in order to promote alternative identities. But why do they choose these names? Ali chose his name because he felt racism had

greatly influenced his life. Maybe 50 Cent feels that money has influenced him. Maybe L.L. Cool J felt that cool influenced him.

7. For this assignment, create a Web site that uses images and text to identify several influences on your life. These influences may come from popular culture, religion, family, school, history, science, or some other area.

 After making this Web site, find a pattern that connects these influences. From that pattern, give yourself a new name. For instance, in *The Autobiography of Malcolm X*, Malcolm X describes racism as the pattern under-lining his influences. Racism led him to X-out his white name, Little.

 Expand your Web site so that it demonstrates, through your influences, how you came to choose this new name. The expansion should, in fact, act as an alternative autobiography. By following your choices, we should be able to understand why you chose your new name. Think of how you can use hyperlinks to demonstrate your choice through a variety of fragmented pages and images.

 The purpose of the autobiography is not to say where you came from or where you were born, but rather how a specific pattern of influences has led you to choose a new name.

8. A discussion about the black male is, in fact, a discussion about identity. We use cultural markers to identify others and ourselves. On the Web, the home page is typically a place where we identify ourselves. My name is X, I'm from X, I'm interested in X (fill in X with your own experience). For this assignment, we want you to rethink how you use the home page to rhetorically identify yourself.

 Just as Muhammad Ali used language to redefine his role as a black male in white America, create a homepage where you use HTML, JavaScript, DHTML, and other tools you can think of to redefine yourself.

 How does the technology allow us new ways to present our self-images? Can we use hyperlinks to create an interlinked self-description (that is, a place where our interests and opinions are interlinked so that they represent who we are)? Can we use hyperlinks to identify ourselves by presenting other Web sites? Can we use scripts that force reader interaction to make readers of our home page contribute to our identities? For instance, could you use a script that allows the reader of your site to fill out a form, and the contents of that form then appear within a self-description you've created on the site? There are many possibilities here. In order to find useful scripts, use the various online resources we pointed out in the preceding chapter or those linked to from this book's Web site.

Chapter

Attitude

Cool Pose

This chapter will take the preceding chapter a step further by examining how cool functions rhetorically as a method of self-expression. Rather than think of cool expression as "whatever you feel like saying," we'll look at specific rituals and symbols that have been associated with cool expression. Since writing is the form of expression we are most concerned with, we'll then apply these items to our continuing efforts to work with hypertext.

In her book *What Is Cool? Understanding Black Manhood in America*, Marlene Kim Connor describes the African-American male experience as one of need. Through a combination of interviews with teenage and young African-Americans about what cool means to them and firsthand accounts of inner city life, Connor arrives at the conclusion that black males need to create a powerful self-image of cool in order to defend themselves against discrimination. In fact, Connor outlines her claim by presenting cool as a set of rituals for the black male. In Connor's argument, the unwelcome environment of street life forces black males to create rituals that may even be detrimental to their own welfare. Regardless of cool's positive or negative influence, Connor sees its purpose as one of survival and need.

Rituals, like myths, are those practices we create to make sense of the world or to establish a livable situation. Religions tend to have very elaborate rituals for holidays, weddings, or coming of age ceremonies. A typical American elementary and secondary school ritual is saying the Pledge of Allegiance early in the day before school officially starts. A typical religious ritual is to say a prayer before one goes to sleep so that one's sleep will be protected.

For Connor, black male rituals include:

- Establishing a sense of manhood through image. This includes creating an image of toughness by wearing specific clothes, jewelry, or headgear.
- Altering English and creating new words to express the uniqueness of black experience. This activity resembles what we've seen in gangsta rap. Two

examples Connor includes are *dis* and *ig*. We might add to her list: *phat*, *fly*, and *Benjamin*, among others.

- Framing symbols of black experience out of fashion, consumer culture, and music. This includes the type of clothes one wears, the various symbols (Mercedes Benz, Volkswagen) one adopts as fashion, and the kinds of music one listens to. These symbols allow users to rethink experience through capitalism. In this sense, the symbol replaces any financial lack, even if that lack becomes fulfilled mythically.

We can understand Connor's claims within the context of much of what we've explored throughout the previous chapter. Cool creates an image, yet that image anchors daily life into specifically shaped relationships for certain parts of our culture. In this way, image plays a powerful role. Image allows cultural participants the means to construct new meanings. As we saw in gangsta rap, image creates a mythology that redefines social life.

> What kind of images do teenagers create when they wear specific clothes like bandanas, nylon head coverings, or jewelry made from automobile insignias? How do these clothing items create a distinct image? What other items play an important role in youth displays of personal image?
>
> What items play an important roles in your life? What rituals do you participate in so that you can feel a part of a social group?
>
> Your class may test the validity of Connor's claim by demonstrating or describing the various rituals you participate in. Does everyone feel that each ritual is meaningful? If one classmate finds a ritual to be superficial, why? If another finds it meaningful, why?

Connor states that, while many of these rituals may seem disturbing or counter-intuitive to the dominant culture, they are survival tools for street life. They allow certain individuals the ability to make meaning for themselves, to, in essence, construct their own rhetoric of survival. This rhetoric, Connor claims, results from social oppression and leads to an inward emotional repression called cool. Consequently, this repression materializes in the form of these various rituals, which, at times, conflict with the dominant culture's accepted norms of behavior.

Put together, these rituals Connor describes produce what the writers Richard Majors and Janet Mancini Billson call, in their book of the same name, the "cool pose." Like Connor's characterization of cool as the series of rituals that meets need and survival demands, Majors and Mancini Billson's cool pose involves black culture's rhetorical presentations of itself to the public. The cool pose, these authors write, creates an attitude that allows African-American males to cope with their marginal status in the culture. Disenchanted and shut out from mainstream society, African-Americans use cool as a tool for creating meaning in their lives. This activity includes the same types of things Connor calls the rituals of cool. But it also includes the establishment of a physical and mental front, a way of preventing emotional feelings from escaping and being freely expressed. In this way, the saying "playing it cool" makes sense. If you play it cool, you hold in your emotions. You play a front. You create a cool pose. Some of the points the authors make to describe the cool pose include:

- Playing it cool—creating a tough exterior to hide inner emotions
- Staying in control—not allowing any aspect of one's behavior to be out of check
- Being tough—always being ready for a fight if necessary
- Participating in violence—demonstrating aggression and physical prowess equals complete masculinity

These attitudes and postures encapsulate much of the physical styles of some of the previous chapter's examples, like gangsta rap and boxing. To put on a cool pose, the authors claim, one creates a self-defining shelter for dealing with life's hardships and injustices.

Look back to the images you may have collected through the exercise in the previous chapter that asked you to search for photos of artists like Nas or L.L. Cool J. In your images, do you see men with their heads tilted and their arms folded? Is this a cool pose? Would you call this fronting? If so, fronting what? Once again, locate the cover image of Public Enemy's *It Takes a Nation of Millions to Hold Us Back*. The album cover places two of the band's members behind the bars of a prison cell. Notice the distant look in their faces, their heads held up as if in defiance. Is this a cool pose? Does being in prison emphasize the cool pose? Why or why not? Why would they use prison as a symbol to hide behind? What does it mean that they put themselves behind prison bars? What we see in these examples is a way of making meaning by rhetorically projecting an attitude.

Do a search for similar examples of cool pose, or look for visualizations of what you think the cool pose should display. Make note of similarities and differences among your examples. Does the image of cool pose extend outward from African-American experience? In other words, can it be generalized to other behaviors or ethnic groups?

The cool pose, therefore, involves taking on alternative attitudes. In creating a cool pose, one, in effect, wears a mask. This metaphorical mask represents distance and dissatisfaction with mainstream culture, often so that the individual appears tough and in charge of him or herself. We might consider the home page, the electronic marker of identity, as a place where the cool pose can transfer into hypertextual writing. In a previous chapter, you were asked to recreate your identity though HTML and related scripts. At the end of this chapter, an exercise asks you to write your identity on your home page via the cool pose.

In their analysis of cool pose, these authors provide us with another method for writing about cool: field research. Most of their insight comes from interviews with various teenagers. When we gather information on specific cultural groups, and when we do so through both observation of these groups and through personal interviews, we call this practice ethnography. We can offer a simple definition of ethnography: the study and description of ethnic cultures so that we can understand the group from its own viewpoint. Through interviews, daily interaction, and observation, ethnographers attempt to understand a group's daily practices. Ethnographers, in theory, also attempt to maintain a sense of distance between themselves and their subject matter. In a sense, ethnographers attempt to keep a "cool" position regarding the groups they study; they strive to be detached and noninvolved in their subjects' lives. Only through detachment can ethnographers separate their own beliefs from the beliefs of the group they study. This is no easy feat, and we might even argue it is impossible, for we are always subject to our beliefs. Nevertheless, we can consider how our impressions of cool often derive from ethnographic research.

Borrowing from Connor as well as Majors and Mancini Billson's work, we can apply some principles of ethnography to cool writing. Doing so allows us to adapt these writers' *methodology*. Methodology simply means how we do something. Without calling it methodology, we've been proposing various methods of cool writing throughout this book. Ethnography offers one more type of methodology. Some methods specific to ethnography include:

- Examining people in the places they work and live, not in unfamiliar locales.
- Attempting to see the studied group from its own point of view. In other words, the ethnographers' personal feelings should be absent, even if the activity studied seems disagreeable to the researcher.
- Keeping detailed records of studied group's behavior, conversations, and places of habitation.
- Making note of any repeated occurrences or behaviors. Patterns reveal important information about the group studied.
- Using deductive reasoning to arrive at a conclusion about the group studied. Deductive reasoning means drawing a conclusion from the data accumulated throughout the research.

While this is a watered-down description of ethnography, it does reflect how those who do ethnographies of cool apply its principles. In their study of cool, Majors and Mancini Billson follow these guidelines fairly completely. They limit their field observations to:

- What people wear
- How people talk
- How people act
- What people do with their leisure time
- What people buy
- What kinds of entertainment people enjoy

Based on their observations of these activities within the African-American community, the authors of *Cool Pose* develop their theory. In other words, the authors develop their claim, or we might call it "their topic sentence," after they have gathered and examined their research. The claim comes second, not first.

The authors begin with a general concept:

What is it about behavior and African-American youth that seems interesting?

And after exploring the question through research and field study, they arrive at a conclusion:

African-American youth construct a cool pose in order to deal with cultural oppression and discrimination.

This, in turn, is another aspect of the authors' methodology for developing the claim of their project: Begin with a generalization, and through research, narrow it to a claim. This kind of conclusion runs contrary to some writing instruction that asks you to form a claim first, then research and support the claim in the body of your essay. We're not suggesting that one method works better than the other, but rather that deductive reasoning allows us first to work around a generalized idea. Only after thinking through our research and notes do we come up with the claim.

The type of writing Connor and Majors and Mancini Billson perform in their study of cool might also be called documentary writing. In effect, the writers document community lives in order to analyze cool's relationship to localized groups. Formal documentary films attempt to capture a specific moment as if it is occurring before the audience's eyes. When we call ethnography documentary, we don't mean to imply they are equal in this way. But they share similarities. Both attempt to explore a given topic as if the writers have no involvement in how the topic is written about or presented. Because the authors in this chapter document cool through ethnography, we might ask if cool itself can function as a kind of documentary. Can we perform a cool documentary; that is, can we create a documentary which uses cool writing (all the methods we are learning in this book) to document a given moment or group? It's a challenging question that some of the following assignments address in various ways.

Further Reading

Mancini Billson, Janet and Richard Majors. *Cool Pose: The Dilemmas of Black Manhood in America*. New York: Lexington Books, 1992.

Connor, Marlene Kim. *What Is Cool? Understanding Black Manhood in America*. Crown Publishers, Inc., 1995.

Pountain, Dick and David Robbins. *Cool Rules: Anatomy of An Attitude*. London: Reaktion, 2000.

Web Site

The *Writing About Cool* Web site includes links to online documentaries you can visit for further inspiration regarding the assignments below.

Class Discussion

1. As a class, make a list of all the figures you consider cool. How many are men? How many are women?
2. What cultural assumptions do we typically make about men and women's ability to influence social behavior? What kind of influences do we normally believe men have on us? How do we treat women? Do we stereotype people based on their gender? Can we imagine a woman athlete to be as influential as Michael Jordan? Why or why not? Has there ever been one?
3. What kind of documentaries are you familiar with? How do documentaries organize information? How much of a documentary is informative and historical; how much is argumentative? Are documentaries *actual* representations of real live events and people? Or are they constructions?

Exercises

1. *The Cool Home Page.* As a follow-up to an assignment in the previous chapter, create a home page that is, in effect, a cool pose. The cool pose involves personal distance. This exercise, therefore, asks you to not write much text so that you can persuade via authorial distance.

   To complete this exercise, you will have to remove any element of emotion, vulnerability, or personable qualities. Like the icon assignment earlier in this book, you should use images—and related JavaScripts that allow you and readers to interact with the images—to describe yourself.

   Similar to Majors and Mancini Billson's methodology, described earlier in this chapter, your image choices should reflect what you think, wear, say, and believe. But you should be able to convey these ideas rhetorically without text or too much text.

2. *The Cool Documentary.* This assignment asks you to use the Web as a medium for documentary production. Documentaries, like ethnographies, tend to depict real life situations as if the viewer is receiving the events as they occur. The writers we've briefly touched upon in this last section treat their work on cool as if they are engaging in documentary work. By studying human behavior and reporting their findings without much editorial influence, they believe they are objectively portraying youth attitudes about cool.

   For this assignment, make a Web documentary on what a given popular culture word means to a given population. For example, the authors of *What Is Cool?* and *Cool Pose* focus on the word cool. The reason for discussing cool, however, stems from their observations. They recognize cool as important to African-American culture after they have studied the cultural group. So don't begin with a term in mind. First study the group. Then, after you have gathered research, find a word or term that repeatedly circulates within the group.

What can you examine? Look to local groups (skateboarders, sororities, fraternities, clubs, city commissioners, teachers, local politicians, employees of a specific store) for material to construct your documentary.

Your documentary should function like an ethnography. Research the group's history. Interview its past and current members. Provide background on the term you've chosen and how its meanings change as your chosen group adopts it.

When you put your work up on the Web, how will you present it? Will you use frames or tables to divide various subjects you've interviewed? Will you hyperlink relevant interviews or observations? Could you have an online interview section? You could create such a section with a script that allows users to fill out a form.

Think beyond simply uploading your information as you would typically write it out in print form. Use some of the cool rhetorical strategies we've discussed so far.

3. *Webography*. This assignment asks you to adapt the methods of these same authors in order to construct a Webography. What is a Webography? A Webography is an ethnography of the Web.

In order to do an ethnography of the Web, you will need to spend a considerable amount of time studying various Web sites, the communities they support, and the behaviors they encourage or work against.

Keep track of all of your notes and research by opening a free Weblog account at Blogger.com. The *Writing About Cool* Web site provides further information regarding how to set up an account at Blogger.com. Weblogs allow you to keep an ongoing online journal of your work. As a class, you will also be able to read each other's notes and learn from each other's methods throughout the assignment.

You may also want to become involved in a listserv or Usenet community. Listservs are e-mail discussion lists categorized around a given topic. You can find many listservs at PAML's index: http://www.taronga.com/cgi-bin/paml_search/

Usenets are online discussion groups. Google's large index of Usenet groups is the most popular at: http://groups.google.com/

On a Web site, demonstrate the conclusions you find. What pattern emerges in your research? What does your ethnography tell you about the Web? The Web is such a vast place of activity that no two projects will look alike or reach the same conclusion.

4. *The Dictionary Assignment*. Connor teaches us that cool involves inventing new words to accommodate contemporary situations (like surviving in the inner city). Online, many sites devoted to hip-hop, for instance, create their own online dictionaries. The purpose of these dictionaries is not just to define slang terms, but to provide cultural contexts for how these terms can be used.

Create your own online dictionary. Frame your dictionary within your ethnic, religious, disciplinary (what you're studying) or professional (where you work or want to work) experience. Use hyperlinks to connect the various terms of your dictionary so that readers will see your text as more than a listing of words and definitions. Allow the hyperlinks to show that these words are related to one another and when used together produce a specific discourse.

You may also want to locate and appropriate a script that will allow users of your site to contribute their own terms to your dictionary. Check with *Writing About Cool's* Web site for further information regarding where you might locate such scripts.

5. *The Handbook of Cool.* Handbooks are teaching tools. Most likely you are using a grammar handbook in your writing class or you have used a handbook for some other purpose: fixing an appliance, seeing a country on a few dollars a day, learning another language. Handbooks accumulate a large amount of information that typically is scattered in a variety of places and put that information under one book for easy reference.

For this project, you will do the same by creating a handbook of cool. And you will put it in hypertext.

For your handbook, you will need to first make an inventory of all the points related to cool we've discussed so far. You will also need to follow up on the recommended readings and other outside research to complement what we haven't covered.

The material we have covered somewhat discusses how to be cool. But for the most part, we're concerned with how to use cool to write. This means cool can be used to teach someone how to do something else.

Then plan how you will structure your handbook. Use another handbook as a model (a writing handbook, a handbook for fixing the sink, a handbook for seeing Europe on $25 a day, etc.). What points will you discuss? Will you provide visual examples? Step by step instructions?

How will you use hyperlinks to aid in the reading of your handbook? Will there be a menu on every page? Will you use frames and have a menu on the side or top of the page?

In the end, readers should be able to get from your handbook an idea of not how to be cool, but how to use cool to create something else.

6. *The Handbook of X.* Do the same project again, only instead of doing a handbook of cool, write a handbook of X. X can be any term from:

The discipline you are studying
Popular culture
History
Science
Sports, etc.

The idea is to demonstrate through research and accumulation of the term's multiple applications how this word can teach us to do something outside of its familiar purpose. Find multiple meanings of the word across various areas and demonstrate how their juxtaposition produces a new usage of the term.

Chapter

10

Literature

In the previous chapters, we've examined cool in relationship to the World Wide Web, advertising, music, and popular culture. In this chapter, we'll focus on literature. In particular, we'll examine how the idea of cool has been discussed in various poems and novels. Just as these other areas of discourse offer examples of cool, literature does as well. What we'll attempt to learn from specific literary texts, however, is how they teach us additional ways cool constructs language and how such language can be applied to electronic writing.

What do we mean, though, by literature? What constitutes the category we associate with literature? Chances are you've taken (or will take) courses in the English department of your college or university in which the word literature was employed to describe the semester's readings. You might have been required to take an Introduction to Literature or a Survey of Literature course. What made the texts you read in these courses so special that they were defined as literary? What kinds of stories, poems, and novels do we consider to be literature, and what other kinds do we not consider to be literature? Does the definition of literature depend on who creates the distinction between literary and nonliterary? In other words, is a book or a poem literary because it has been taught in a college classroom (school, then, creates the definition of literature)? Or is the same work literature because the word "literature" has been printed in the upper left-hand corner of the back cover (the publisher of the book, in this case, creates the definition)? Does studying literature make us better individuals? Why or why not? Does literature have specific stylistics that make it easily identifiable? Or is it just one of those things that recognize when we see?

Make a list of the characteristics you typically ascribe to literary works. Which of the following items appear on your list?

- Includes novels, short stories, essays, plays, and poems
- Connects cultural values and ideas

- Asks questions regarding human experience
- Provides readers places to think about larger life issues
- Involves an understanding of human psyche and behavior

What else might we include in a list of literary attributes? Are there specific rhetorical strategies we associate with literature? If so, which? Our job in this chapter is to explore this latter point in relationship to cool.

We began this book with an examination of the word cool and the promise to explore its various meanings, and we can position the term literature in the same way. Literature maintains distinct meanings dependent on context and place. In the past, you might have heard literature categorized as "timeless," "uplifting," "universal," or some other loosely defined association that really doesn't bring us any closer to specifying which texts should be considered literature and which shouldn't. If we believe, for example, that literature is uplifting, what about novels that are depressing or haunting for their troubling descriptions? If we state that literature is universal, what do we do then when one cultural text is ignored while another cultural text is favored? If we can agree that cool creates a multitude of definitions and understandings, then can we also agree that words like literature do the same?

Which one of these writers exemplifies a literary figure?

- William Shakespeare
- John Milton
- Ernest Hemingway
- Charles Bukowski
- Alice Walker
- Maxine Hong Kingston
- Ishmael Reed

If you don't recognize some of the names, look them up. Why do some of these names stand out for you, and why do some not? Does literature mean name recognition? Is it like brand-name recognition, similar to what we saw with Nike? On the other hand, is it possible for readers to always recognize every name of every writer? Does a lack of recognition indicate a lack of literary status? If we reduce literature to name recognition, then are we saying that literature is no different than popular culture, and so its basis derives from the ways we daily interact with its production? How will you respond if the literary figures represented in this section of the book don't appear familiar to you?

We don't have any one answer for these questions. As we explore the relationship between literature and cool, however, we don't want to claim literature creates any sense of truth or beauty. Why not? What's wrong with aspiring to ideal states of consciousness and value like truth or beauty? Terms like truth and beauty are too ambiguous to use as qualifiers for labeling literary works. What one person classifies as truth, another dismisses. As we've seen previously, cultural values create such distinctions, and such values vary from group to group and situation to situation. The same holds for aesthetic categories like beauty. To claim a novel as universally beautiful or pleasing proves problematic when we realize that such distinctions are based on taste. If you recall our discussion on popular culture, we asked you to place aside your personal tastes while we examined various movements in popular culture. The same applies to literature. The study of texts as a step towards exploring cultural meanings or discursive practices is not about being entertained or about personally relating to situations or characters. Instead, we want to treat literary texts as tools that can teach us new ways to create meaning and knowledge.

Our task in this chapter will not be to hold up a poem or novel as exemplary of great beauty. Nor will we dissect intricate meanings of texts to decipher their usage of metaphor or symbolism. Then why are we going to look at literature? To answer this question, we ask another question: What does literature have to do with writing?

All literary texts are, in effect, writing. They consist of words and images whose purpose is to convey some sense of meaning. Literary texts, however, apply writing differently. One novelist may fragment her work into various sections; one may write a linear document. One poet may cut up sentences and use slang; one may use grammatically correct syntax and punctuation. Various writers employ various writing strategies in assembling texts. Such is the nature of rhetoric's relationship to literature.

To understand how literature constructs meaning, we want to ask how a poem or novel is rhetorically constructed. What does the work do in terms of its production of expression? How does it use language? How does it use imagery? What specific features of rhetoric does it employ? How can we adapt some of these methods for our own writing, not to be creative writers, but to be rhetorically meaningful? And how does all of this relate to cool?

We also don't have the space in this textbook to read together in detail the poems or novels discussed. Consequently, we assume that our general overviews of the selected works give you enough background to consider how cool functions in these texts. We also assume that you will pursue further readings of these works on your own in order to better grasp the points we make. Check this book's Web site as well for links to online versions of some of the texts discussed in this chapter or for more information regarding the writers discussed in this chapter.

Our choices for literary works might seem arbitrary to you. Our reasons for choosing the texts you will read about stem from two areas of literary study that we feel are appropriate to cool: African-American literature and Beat writings. Our selections from each area are not meant to be inclusive. The purpose of this chapter and the following one is not to anthologize in a comprehensive manner. Instead, we hope to offer a brief survey of a few relevant texts. You should follow up what we touch upon by consulting the recommended readings at the end of the chapter. Just like the other areas we've studied, we'll treat each text as a lesson in cool writing.

Postwar Cool—African-American Literature

As we've seen already, post–World War II America brought significant changes in African-American culture. Moreover, such changes shaped a newfound influence of African-American culture on mainstream, white America. Notably, the advancement of the movement for racial equality increased as new voices made themselves heard in the political and social arenas. Like Malcolm X, Martin Luther King, Jr., and Amiri Baraka, poets and writers also searched for ways to explain the quest for equality. Often, their ideas clashed with earlier publicly endorsed modes of thought. This conflict included questioning how one creates expression as social protest. At other times, their works represented the internal paradoxes that result from attempting to classify a race's position as unified. While African-American writers chose many contexts and approaches, we'll focus on how two poets chose the subject of cool. We'll also examine a white novelist's interest in cool, particularly because his graphic description of inner city life has often resulted in a misidentification of his identity as African-American.

Haki Madhubuti (Don Lee)

Haki Madhubuti's poetry gives us an example of how cool has been used in literature to define and critique African-American experience. Madhubuti (whose original name was Don Lee), an African-American poet interested in language construction as well as social activism, belonged to a group of influential 1960s writers who attempted to create racial awareness through their work. In 1973, he adopted the name Haki Madhubuti, which is Swahili for "Justice, Awakening Strong." Through this action, Lee, like Muhammad Ali, redefined himself as a political act. Adopting a new Swahili name conjures African heritage over the American upbringing English names convey. By doing so, Lee reminded audiences of the power of language; the very act of naming oneself maintains as much importance as naming an event or location.

> If you completed the Autobiography of _____ exercise in Chapter 8, compare the new name you gave yourself with the name Don Lee adopted. Why did you choose your name and why did Lee choose his? What rhetorical actions were involved in each choice?

For our purposes, we'll look closely at Lee's poem "But He Was Cool, or: He Even Stopped for Green Lights" in order to locate specific rhetorical strategies we can use in our own writing On this book's accompanying Web site, you can find a link to an online version of this poem. A poem about African-American identity, the work immediately draws attention to cool's role in African-American daily life. The poem carefully describes an African-American male figure, who, as described by the poem's title, was so cool he would stop for green lights (instead of only stopping for red, as is common practice). The figure, then, is cool for his transgression, for breaking the rules. This male is described as:

> super-cool
> ultrablack
> a tan/purple
> had a beautiful shade

If American cultural perception determines blackness as an embodiment of cool, this male meets the criteria. He's "ultrablack," meaning his appearance goes beyond the typical shades of black associated with African-American identity; his is "pure" and "true" to black cultural identity. He's also dressed in African garb and speaks Swahili and Yoruban. Thus, this figure maintains a connection with the "motherland" Africa and knows his roots. Rather than wearing a t-shirt and jeans, he wears "beads" and "imported sea shells," items supposedly related to African folkloric practices. After the poem's initial tone explains the male figure as authentically black and as in touch with his heritage, the narrator of the poem proceeds to describe this man as:

> cool-cool is so cool he was un-cooled by other niggers' cool
> cool-cool ultracool was bop-cool/ice box cool so cool cold cool
> his wine didn't have to be cooled, him was air conditioned cool
> cool-cool/real cool made me cool—now ain't that cool
> cool-cool so cool him nick-named refrigerator.

Notice the repetition of the same word, cool. What context does each usage of cool serve? All the references don't convey to the same activity. Consider the first line of this description:

> cool-cool is so cool he was un-cooled by other niggers' cool

Lee begins with a statement of cool we are mostly familiar with: something or someone embodies the feeling we describe as cool. But the next part of the line states that this man was "un-cooled" by others' display of cool. What does Lee mean by this play on words? And why does he choose the word "nigger" here? This word typically communicates a racial epithet. How is it used in this line? Is its usage meant as derogatory, as a racist declaration? Or does "other niggers" imply that the figure we're hearing about is one too, yet in a positive way? How could this term be used positively? And how does this meaning fit with what we earlier described as the cool pose?

Where else is the word "nigger" used in a nondiscriminatory manner? How, for example, is the term (with slightly different spelling) used in hip-hop culture? Given its problematic past as a racial epithet, why is it used at all?

How can a word be racist in one situation and not in another? Does the word still evoke discomfort? If so, why has it been adapted for specific contexts? These are questions specific to rhetoric. Using a word for one context causes discomfort; in another context it doesn't. Think about and discuss the differences.

Look closer at the second and third lines in the selection quoted above. Is this poem starting to play with words for a humorous effect? Note the references to keeping wine cool or being like air conditioning. And when the narrator moves to the next line, we discover that this figure is so cool he makes the narrator cool! Cool rubs off one person onto another. No longer an emotional state, cool becomes like a rash.

What are we to make from these puns? Has the tone changed? How seriously does the narrator take the figure he describes? First, we hear about a man who understands his relationship to a motherland through his speech and dress. Then the tone of the poem shifts as this figure becomes a caricature, a series of metaphors that pun on cool as laid back and "with it" to being cold. How does the narrator use humor to transform the tone of the poem's approach to coolness? How do the puns function rhetorically?

Finally, the poem's narrator states that even though this male personifies cool because of his dress, speech, and attitude, he remains ignorant about recent riots in major American inner cities:

cool-cool so cool
he didn't know,
after detroit, newark, chicago &c.,
we had to hip

Political issues take a back seat to fashion choices. Making this point clear, the narrator switches from an elaboration of coolness to one of blackness. The narrator claims that not knowing about African-American strife echoes the sentiments of cool. Cool equals political ignorance. Having political awareness equals blackness. The poem concludes with:

to be black
is
to be
very-hot

In the end of the poem, coolness marks a state of image. It creates a game where supposed cool dress and attitude bear little consequence for political action, which, in the end, matters more than fashion. Being involved in national politics, which for the time period of this poem means the late 1960s struggle for civil rights, is hot. How does this view differ from or complement any previous discussions of cool we've encountered?

- Using this poem as your basis, make a list with two headings: Coolness and Blackness. Under each term, list qualities you feel match that idea. Base your assumptions on how each is typically portrayed and represented in American culture. Go online and find representations that demonstrate each point rhetorically.
- Choose two other words, one popular, one ethnic, that function similarly. See if you can repeat the same process.
- Choose a different word as descriptive of someone you know (either someone close to you or famous). See if you can pun the word the way Lee puns cool. Lee's punning has a rhetorical purpose, to offset the frivolous nature of cool as image with the seriousness of being black during difficult civil strife. In general, therefore, punning has rhetorical purposes. When you do the exercises at the end of this chapter (or elsewhere in this book), think about how you can use hyperlinks to replicate the punning process. Hyperlinks can be used in an associative way (click on this meaning of the word and you are taken to a similar or related meaning). Can they also be used for punning, the way Lee uses poetry to pun? On this book's Web site, you'll find some more examples of using hyperlinks to pun.

Gwendolyn Brooks

Gwendolyn Brooks is another African-American poet who wrote about African-American community and experience. She began working in the mid-1940s and wrote until her death in 2000. Brooks, a Pulitzer Prize winner for poetry, tackled difficult social issues in her work regarding black culture and oppression. She often described the lives of inner city youth or militant activists in her work. Her poem "We Real Cool" serves this section of the chapter. The poem focuses briefly on several pool hall players. The first line of the poem creates its setting through a distinct title, separate from the poem itself. The poem, in its entirety, reads:

The Pool Players. Seven at the Golden.

We real cool. We
Left school. We

Lurk late. We
Strike straight. We

Sing sin. We
Thin gin. We

Jazz June. We
Die soon.

Notice the poem's overall inclusiveness. An undefined "we" determines each set of actions. The first question the poem asks, then, is where is the border between the reader and the narrator? Who makes up this general "we"? Does "we" refer to all of us or a specific group of people talking about themselves? What is the rhetorical effect of making one's writing inclusive?

Before we go through the poem, by breaking off each portion of the poem, we can divide its attributes of cool into several sections:

- Education
- Rebellion
- Violence
- Sexuality
- Alcohol and drug abuse
- Carefree attitude
- Consequences

Brooks breaks down cool into very traditional sections, descriptions we've encountered throughout this book. While these topics are typical to interchanges regarding cool, Brooks uses them in a unique way. Let's discuss each area separately in order to understand how Brooks rhetorically creates the idea of cool. Use this discussion as both a way to understand Brooks' poem and as a method you can employ as well in your writing.

A considerable amount of the brief imagery Brooks employs plays off of cultural assumptions regarding teenage lifestyles. And as we've seen previously in this book (and we'll see in subsequent chapters), cool is very much about making and breaking assumptions.

Brooks begins the poem with a statement about cool and education: "We real cool/we left school." Think about your own impressions of school when you were in high school. School represents the opposite of cool; its structure and set of rules and orders conflict with cool's rebelliousness. Why does school maintain this image for youth?

- Make a list of all the movies you've seen where teenagers place themselves in conflict with the school system.
- Such films might include *The Breakfast Club*, *Ferris Bueller's Day Off*, or *American Pie*. Typically, the teachers and principal stand on one side of the good versus bad spectrum, the students on the other.
- As we go through the poem, compare how such films match Brooks' descriptions.

In the second section of the poem, "We lurk late" indicates a sense of rebelliousness. Curfews dictate when teenagers can roam freely at night and when they must return to their homes. By lurking late, the youth who are the focus of this poem break such regulations. The second part of this section, "We strike straight," implies that staying out late leads to violent behavior. To be cool late at night involves being tough and prepared for late-night encounters. Think back to the cool pose image in order to visualize this moment more completely. Think of the stereotypical image of teenage gangs roaming the streets late at night. How accurate are such images? And if they maintain any degree of accuracy, are these universal images or images specific to certain locales and economic situations?

"We sing sin/We thin gin," the next section reads. Do you think that sexual activity (here represented by the idea of "sin") and alcohol usage ("gin") are related in any way? Why does Brooks tie the two areas together? Notice how this section leads into the poem's conclusion: "We jazz June/We die soon." Does sexual promiscuity and alcohol usage lead to both good times (jazzing) and death? How have we moved from being cool to dying soon? Like Madhubuti's poem, Brooks' work changes tone from its beginning to its end. While it starts with what feels to be an embracement of cool, "We real cool," it concludes with a negative feeling, "We die soon." What happens when we remove all of the middle sections and leave only this beginning and end? How does that affect our reading of the poem?

How does this poem work from popular understandings of cool as urban attitude constructed to create the image of someone who is too fast to live/too young to die? Can you build a list of popular culture figures who match this description? In Madhubuti's poem, the cool figure favors image over political awareness. In Brooks' poem, cool leads to youthful recklessness. Are these writers being fair to cool? Or do they write from specific cultural contexts? What might those contexts include? Urban, inner city approaches to cool most likely differ from those of college students. Why? How do these poems rupture such differences in meaning?

When we break down Brooks' categories of cool (dropout, rebelliousness, violent, sexual, drunk), we see a rhetoric of attitude created. Without actually making a negative statement directly about youth and the image of cool, Brooks situates a few select phrases to create the impression of cool as negative influence. Her rhetoric utilizes limited vocabulary to make a critical gesture. She *fragments* her descriptions, a point you can apply to the exercises at the end of this chapter. And like Madhubuti's poem, Brooks challenges initial assumptions about what cool figures do or look like. To say "We real cool" isn't a good thing in this poem, is it? Likewise, was fashion important for Madhubuti, or was political awareness? Both these poems demonstrate how cool, when dissected, can lead to critique. Think of how you can apply these lessons to your writing:

- Brooks' poem takes place in a bar. What other locales could be used to critique specific cultural attitudes?
- How might you rewrite Brooks' poem by focusing on the university you study in, the place you work, or the industry you aim to join?
- Instead of making cool the initial term that sparks your imagery, what term relevant to the locale you've chosen could initiate the critique?
- What if you chose to critique the World Wide Web for a specific problem or position. What term conducive to this issue could you choose?
- What if you chose to critique the integration of technology in the classroom? What word would you choose to center this critique? Could you perform such a critique in hypertext? How?
- Could you do the same thing in order to critique this book?

Warren Miller

Warren Miller's 1959 *The Cool World* is a novel that graphically depicts the turmoil of Harlem life in the late 1950s. Miller, often considered to be an African-American author because of his detailed portrayal of black culture, was, in fact, a white writer. We include him in this section because a discussion about African-American literature may also include writers who aren't African-American, but whose work reflects or describes African-American experience and culture.

The Cool World depicts its narrator's, Duke, quest to earn enough money to buy a pistol from the drug dealer Priest. In exchange for selling marijuana that Priest supplies, Duke hopes to earn enough money to buy the gun and use it in an upcoming gang fight.

Just as we've condensed Madhubuti's and Brooks' poems to bulleted rhetorical points, we can do the same for Miller's novel. *The Cool World* approaches cool as inner city lifestyle by focusing on:

- Language—the novel utilizes slang throughout its narrative, which is told through the first person narration of Duke. Words are misspelled and written in dialect.
- Violence—the novel's first scene involves the illegal sale of a handgun by Priest to Duke. This activity continues throughout the narrative as a gang war unfolds.
- Despair—the novel's graphic depiction of inner city life is based on descriptions of specific cultural markers that indicate an impoverished neighborhood with no financial prospects.

Miller's language and imagery rhetorically create the idea of cool as black underclass lifestyle. By limiting the inner-city experience to these few traits, Miller reduces cool to a negative attitude (similar to Connor and Majors and Billson's analysis of cool we discussed earlier in this book). Consider this brief passage in which Duke describes his surroundings:

> The street fulla rackets. Evry body on the street bisy survivin an doin this & that to get thru the week and get up the rent an the bread for the super market. (68)

What do you make of the misspelled words? Or the use of & in place of "and"? How does the deliberate alteration of conventional English alter the way you read this passage? Do you imagine an educated person speaking? If your answer is no, why not? What assumptions are you making based on how language is used by various economic classes? Think of the first line of Brooks' poem as you examine this passage. Is this another example of cool attitude as one that is anti-school? The passage continues with a local description of the narrator's environment.

> Mostly the street jus apartment houses an stoops. Long rows facin each other an no space in between excep one place where the building fell down. We had a club house in the ruin for a while but the City come an took away the ruin. It jus full up with junk that place now. (68–69)

From this passage, let's pose a number of problematic questions the reading raises. What kind of place does this passage describe? How does Miller convey a sense of despair through his imagery? Do you imagine the apartment buildings appear different and express individuality? Or are they uniform, an expression of mass conformity? Why would all the buildings look the same; why isn't there architectural variation? How far apart are the buildings? What do the cramped living conditions tell you about this neighborhood? What do you imagine people doing on the stoops? If the block consists of only apartments and stoops, most likely there are few places to go for entertainment. We can imagine neighbors sitting restless on the stoops with little to do. What role does the government (the City) play in maintaining a status quo of despair? How does the government deal with the dilapidation of recreational facilities? We need to consider why it's important for Duke to narrate his surroundings this way.

Let's compare this depiction with several other place descriptions in the novel. The first comes from the novel's beginning:

> Water truck come by then an slick the street. All the crap pushed into the gutters garbage boxes butts bottles cundums news papers all hissin an skewin into the gutters. (9)

The next passage also comes early in the narration:

> The project has a little elevator like a telephone booth the green walls all scratched with initials an you know things. An it smell like garbage. New bilding but it got the Uptown stink. (20)

Consider the objects Miller uses to demonstrate the feeling of cool as despair. Which items does he place in the streets of Harlem? Why these and not others? What kinds of meanings do we associate with "bottles," "cundums," and loose, scattered "news papers" floating around in the street? Miller's novel often depicts social surroundings as related to the emotions of its characters. Thus, if we read about how the neighborhood is a place of despair, we can see similar parallels in the characters. Living in a cramped environment with little to do and no opportunity for work or recreation, people's tensions rise. This next scene describes the anticipation of violence. Notice how Duke describes himself regarding an expected violent moment.

> So I be walkin home like a hotshot but looking allatime right left in evry doorway. Closer I get to my house the more I get a feelin. I get a feelin they are out and waiten. First I think Maybe it will be at the hardware store. An I come up on my toes. Walkin soft. Blade in my hand. I am cool. I am cool. Man but my goddamn heart wont stop poundin. (26)

Cool signifies the moment where one responds to fear, where one plays it cool, puts on a cool pose, acts indifferent to trepidation. *The Cool World* is a place of fear. Notice how this attitude is created in the following passage:

> They ain't law on the streets. No an none in the houses. You ask me why an I tellin you why we do whut we have to do. Because when they ain't law you gotta make law. Other wise evry thing wild Man an you don't belong an you alone. No body want that I dont care who are a doctor or whut ever you are I dont care. No body want that.

So we go in the gang. We start hanging aroun an become a junior an then we grow up some more an go takin in the gang. Then we belong an we part of the thing an not scared out on the edge. (149–150)

Think about this passage in juxtaposition with Chapter 8's discussion of gangsta rap. How does this attitude reflect the excerpts of lyrics we read? At what point do we take this type of language at face value, and at what point do you question it as just another example of cool pose, a front to hide fear and anxiety?

Find a song that describes a physical location. Make a listing of all of the specific markers the song uses to make its imagery felt. Do these images function as icons (see our previous discussion)? How effective are they at raising audience emotion?

What we can learn from this brief examination of Miller's novel is how cool rhetorically can create a sense of place as well as emotion. Yet, Miller's decision to name his novel *The Cool World*, as well as the novel's emphasis on African-American inner-city life, means that the novel's rhetoric is more than mere setting. Its coolness derives from the ways it positions traditional understandings of cool (violence, rebellion) in a specific geographic location. The exercises following this section will ask you to rhetorically write about place in similar ways.

Further Reading

Brooks, Gwendolyn. *Selected Poems*. New York: Harper and Row, 1963.
Himes, Chester. *If He Hollers Let Him Go*. New York: Thunder's Mouth Press, 1986 (1945).
———. *The Real Cool Killers*. New York: Vintage Crime, 1987 (1959).
Madhubuti, Haki. *Book of Life*. Detroit: Broadside Press, 1969.
———. *Don't Cry, Scream*. Broadside Press, 1969.
Miller, Warren. *The Cool World*. New York: Crest, 1959.
Reed, Ishmael. *Mumbo Jumbo*. New York: MacMillan, 1972.
Wright, Richard. *Lawd Today*. New York: Walker and Company, 1963.

Web Site

Go to this book's Web site and follow the links to related online readings and author information from this chapter.

Class Discussion

1. The poems and novel we discussed in this chapter are specific to African-American culture. What poems or novels are you familiar with that are specific to other racial and ethnic groups? To gendered groups? To college student life? How do such writings establish internal critique?
2. The works in this chapter challenge conventional English structure. We read such works in English classes that maintain strict rules for how students should write "correct" English. As a class, how do you negotiate the differ-

ences between the two? How can a text be deemed literary for using slang and misspellings, but an essay be labeled "incorrect" for doing the same?

3. On a similar note, these texts distort the English language for rhetorical purposes. How might you alter HTML code to do likewise? Brainstorm several possible approaches to this question.

Exercises

1. *The Web Portrait.* The writers we've briefly examined in this chapter focus on developing portraits of the characters they wish to describe as cool. Through the inclusion of specific cultural markers (dress, language, attitude), these writers paint a picture of the cool figure.

    Create a Web portrait that describes a specific individual from your community (local or state). Because the Web allows us to use images and to juxtapose various quotations and textual descriptions, collect a number of these items first to use in your portrait.

    Then create a Web portrait of someone from your school.

    The poems/novel used as examples in this chapter sketch out characters whose traits exemplify different aspects of cool. Your portrait will also exemplify a trait. Because you will write for the Web, your portrait will incorporate images. But its effect will also come from juxtaposed quotations, descriptions, and associated imagery. The purpose is not to create a simple narration of someone (Once there was a man named...), but rather to use images, links, and textual citations as the components of your portrait.

2. *Urban Narrative Project.* Madhubuti, Brooks, and Miller situate cool as an urban feeling. They use specific rhetorical strategies in order to do so. Building off the Web documentary project in Chapter 9, create a Web narrative that describes a local urban community in your area. This community might be the downtown area, a historic neighborhood that has become rundown, a racially divided section of your town or city. But just as these writers use cool as a metaphor to describe urban communities, use one word or image as a central, guiding metaphor. This means that every image you use, every link you create, must be somehow directed by this word or image.

    For this assignment, you might think about how you can incorporate image maps into your project. Can the image map establish a metaphoric relationship to the community you describe similar to what the writers in this chapter accomplish with words?

    Another approach might be to divide your project into frames of various sizes, each highlighting an aspect of the community you wish to emphasize. Or you could do something similar, without the multiple-page interactions frames create, by using tables.

Chapter

The Beats

After World War II, a group of disenfranchised young writers began gathering in New York's Greenwich Village and San Francisco. These writers, who were mostly educated, white, and male, began to rethink their relationship to American culture, to media and technology, and to self-expression. Self-named "the Beats" for their feelings of both despair (feeling beat, low down) and holiness (beatific), these writers started a new movement in American literature concerned with issues of alienation, marginality, dissatisfaction with the status quo, and rebellion. Jack Kerouac, Allen Ginsberg, William S. Burroughs, Gary Snyder, Gregory Corso, and Lawrence Ferlinghetti comprised the core group of the Beats. Each contributed important work to the movement's oeuvre and its attempt to rethink individual relationships to state, educational, and cultural control.

For our purposes, we'll focus on just two of the Beat writers: Jack Kerouac and William S. Burroughs. This selection is not meant to imply that these writers were better than the others or their work more important. Instead, we'll limit our discussion to two influential writers for the sake of space limitations. We'll briefly survey some of Kerouac's and Burroughs' output in order to understand how these writers rhetorically created alternative forms of expression. Just as the Internet currently challenges traditional approaches to writing, the Beats viewed conventional literary forms as unsuitable for what they wanted to say.

In the case of Kerouac and Burroughs, post–World War II advancements in technology as well as shifts in public perception of race and gender necessitated an adjustment of the structure of the novel. Technological innovations in television and radio altered the nature of communication. For writers like Kerouac and Burroughs, the novel's place in the overall communication network appeared outdated. Its form seemed to contrast sharply with new technology's influence on communicative practices. In turn, Kerouac and Burroughs introduced new approaches to the construction of discourse. They often attempted to replicate in their own writings the ways in which technology functions. We'll concentrate on some of the approaches they conceived.

With this in mind, an analogy to contemporary technological innovations, therefore, might seem obvious. What television and radio meant to the 1950s, the Internet means to us today. If 1950s and 1960s writers found themselves rethinking writing in relationship to technological innovations in communication, we might be on similar footing. Following this logic, we, too, need to reevaluate the ways we construct discourse. As you have noticed, this is a central theme to this book's approach to cool. As we survey Kerouac and Burroughs, take note of how their work relates to technology.

We've made a bold claim here: the 1950s and 1960s saw new advancements in technology. Beyond television and radio, what were they? How do technological changes affect *rhetorical* changes?

As you read Kerouac and Burroughs on your own, research what kinds of inventions were appearing during this time period. Focus your research on:

Communications

Computers

Travel

The military

Then see if a correlation exists between these developments and the novels you are reading.

Jack Kerouac

Often credited with creating the term Beat, Kerouac is typically recognized as the founder of the Beat movement. His influential novel *On the Road* describes a group of restless youths' search for higher existence as they travel across country and into Mexico. *On the Road* established Kerouac as a major literary figure because of its unorthodox style and material. It spoke of stark, individual pursuit, openly discussed drug usage, and proposed that the end of the road (i.e., the end of life's search) can be found in a brothel in Mexico. In addition to *On the Road*, Kerouac wrote many other novels. We'll concentrate on two, *The Subterraneans* and *Visions of Gerard*. We recommend, however, that you follow up our discussion by also reading some of Kerouac's other texts.

The Subterraneans takes place in New York's Greenwich Village, a hip urban section of New York City popular with artists, poets, and writers. Like Miller's *The Cool World,* the locale of cool narratives again is the city. Unlike Miller's work, *The Subterraneans* treats city life as the background to emotional tribulations, not racial oppression. Yet like Miller's novel, Kerouac's text complicates the question of race. The narrative explores the interracial relationship between Leo (who is white) and Mardou (who is African-American).

Reading *The Subterraneans*, readers are often struck by its unconventional prose. The sentences run into one another and the ideas quickly switch without much transition. Kerouac called this style *spontaneous writing*, the assumption being that he wrote whatever came to mind as quickly as possible. In retrospect, we have learned that Kerouac's spontaneous prose wasn't very spontaneous; its construction was deliberately crafted with careful editing. Nevertheless, Kerouac offers a rhetoric for a quick-paced writing style. The image of spontaneous writing may be more important than actually writing spontaneously. Why? One reason is that it may comment on a social attitude prevalent at a given time. The speed of technological development occurring in the 1950s and 1960s becomes reflected in the pace of Kerouac's style.

Let's examine the effect of this kind of writing on its audience. First we'll examine some brief passages, then we'll ask you to perform some "spontaneous writing." *The Subterraneans* begins like this:

> Once I was young and had so much more orientation and could talk with nervous intelligence about everything and with clarity and without as much literary preambling as this; in other words, this is the story of an unself-confident man, at the same time of an egomaniac, naturally, facetious won't do—just to start at the beginning and let the truth seep out, that's what I'll do—It began on a warm summernight—ah, she was sitting on a fender with Julien Alexander who is…let me begin with the history of the subterraneans of San Francisco. (1–2)

Take a look at this passage's rhetorical construction. How many times does the narration shift in this brief introduction? How do these shifts take place? Often, novels use the opening sequence to establish a sense of setting or to introduce a main character. Similar to typical classroom writing assignments, the novel's opening is supposed to function as an introduction to what will follow. Yet, how many issues and characters are introduced here without much clarification? Who's speaking? Who was sitting on a fender? Who is Julien Alexander? Who are the subterraneans? Kerouac's notion of spontaneity, then, attempts to recreate a sort of mental rambling, as if we, the readers, are privileged to the inner mind of the narrator. In turn, the rhetorical effect of this type of narrative creates a nonlinear prose that *assumes* audience awareness. Ideas shift from one to the other quickly, often lacking chronological order. Readers must reconstruct for themselves the order of the story.

- Where else do you find nonlinear forms of narrative? Can you think of some specific examples?

This style of writing works from moments of digression. Kerouac's usage of the digression, an aside that alters the narrative's path so that it becomes nonlinear, is a rhetorical point we can learn from when writing for the Web. Asides and breaks in thought can themselves be quite informative and revealing. They also can allow us to move between distinct subject matter in a persuasive manner.

Let's look at one such example in which the novel's main character, Leo, describes first the group of friends he belongs to called the subterraneans, and then suddenly, his girlfriend Mardou's father:

> There we were in all gray San Francisco, of the gray West, you could almost smell rain in the air and far across the land, over the mountains beyond Oakland and out beyond Donner and Truckee was the great desert of Nevada, the wastes leading to Utah, to Colorado, to the cold cold come fall plains where I kept imagining that Cherokee-half-breed hobo father of hers lying bellydown on a flatcar with the wind furling back his rags and black hat, his brown and sad face facing all that land and desolation. (26–27)

Leo begins by mentioning the subterraneans living in San Francisco. Suddenly, his narration switches. What word causes this switch to occur? We might pinpoint "West," for example. Notice how it serves as a catalyst, a trigger for the next thought regarding the smell of rain and the mountains. The image of mountains, then, leads to the Donner expedition in Utah, the nearby state of Colorado, and finally Mardou's father, who is imagined as a wandering hobo riding the rails. This movement transpires as Kerouac uses specific words to fuel additional ideas. From "West," Kerouac eventually constructs an image of a downtrodden man hoping trains for transportation. The nonlinear arrival at this image moves through associations. "West" triggers that series of associations.

Such movements via words operate on an audience's cultural awareness and knowledge. The assumption made in this passage is that you will know that the West served as a place for migrant labor and hobos who traveled around looking for work in the 1920s and 1930s. It also assumes a familiarity with the Donner party as well as the location and history of various western states. But if an audience recognizes the references, a powerful image is created, one that forms an association (Leo in San Francisco with Mardou's father) where one didn't exist previously. If you collect a number of images and words, therefore, you can create a chain of ideas which creates its own nonlinear progression.

Think of this chain-formed of writing as follows:
Image + Related Image + Related Image to the Previous Image + Related Image to the Previous Image…

The chain continues as long as you want to extend the series of related references.

As a class, test Kerouac's method.

Test #1

One person writes down a word, phrase, idea, or feeling. That person passes his/her work to the next person. The second person writes down another word, phrase, idea, or feeling that relates or feeds off of what the first person wrote. Continue this process until everyone has contributed.

Read back the results out loud and see if the composition makes sense.

You can also have several threads of writings going on simultaneously so that no one will sit idle for too long.

Test #2

The class divides up into pairs. One member of the pair says out loud to the partner a personal anecdote ("when I was seven, I broke my brother's favorite **toy**"). The same member writes down what she said.

The other member of the pair takes a word, idea, or phrase from what the first person said, and forms her own anecdote ("all Christmas, I begged my parents to buy me the one **toy** I wanted, the complete Star Wars action figure set"). Then the person who said this statement writes down what she said.

The process continues, each member creating an association from the other member's anecdote. When time is called, all the pairs read out loud what they wrote; in each pair, the members read their associations just as they were said.

For each test, ask what the rhetorical effect is as you listen to the results. What kinds of ideas do you hear? Do you hear ideas you wish were further elaborated? What is the effect of the associations in general?

How could you use hyperlinks in a Web site to replicate this association process?

One place where Kerouac works out a nonlinear approach is in his description of Leo and Mardou's relationship. The nonlinear descriptions of their interracial love affair stirs the narrative to comment on race in complex ways. Moments of affection switch into racial fears and prejudice. Consequently, we can read Kerouac's rhetoric of race as directly related to popular perceptions of racial identity. First, we'll isolate some of the things Leo states about Mardou:

- "At first I had doubts, because she was Negro" (59).
- "I feel that great hepness I'd been having all summer on the street with Mardou my old dream of wanting to be vital, alive like a Negro or an Indian or a Denver Jap or a New York Puerto Rican come true" (96).
- "Every time I see a Mexican gal or Negress I say to myself, 'hustlers,' they're all the same, always trying to cheat and rob you—harking back to all relations of the past with them—Mardou sensing these waves of hostility from me and silent" (129).

Spend some time thinking over these quotations. How do they construct a negative image of African-American women? What kinds of cultural fears and assumptions about African-American women do they play off of? How does the last quotation build off of a negative assumption? Where do such assumptions come from and how do they proliferate in the culture? Refer to the earlier chapter on masculinity and see if there exist connections.

One response to these kinds of passages involves associating Kerouac's personal beliefs with racism. Instead of this approach (which may or may not be true), we need to establish the rhetorical effect of Kerouac's examination of race, the types of words and cultural ideas he utilizes, the ways these words stir readers' emotions. In this way, when we want to understand how rhetoric shapes attitudes, we should concentrate more on how the writer employs language rather than guess at the writer's beliefs.

Is there a rhetoric to racial and gendered assumptions? To help answer that question, undertake the following investigation.

Pick an ethnic group. Pick a gender from that ethnic group. Using the Internet, magazine and newspaper stories, TV shows, songs, advertisements, and other media forms, collect as many references as you can that textually or visually depict your choice.

What kind of patterns do you notice? Do some media forms repeat the same approach to gender and race? Do some of your findings seem similar? Or are they all different?

How do we respond to such representations? Do we ignore them? Do we act upon them? How? Or do we feel that these representations pose no harm to how we conceptualize race and gender? But if that is the case, why are they used with considerable frequency?

The final rhetorical strategy we'll observe in Kerouac's work is nostalgia. Kerouac's novel *Visions of Gerard* treats nostalgia as a tool for organizing its narrative. What is nostalgia? Nostalgia is the activity of longing. Often it involves a romantic reconstruction of past events and feelings in order to wish for their return. Nostalgia replaces the present with an idealized past, even if that past never occurred.

For example, computer technology is sometimes critiqued because it:

- Makes us more distant to one another than we were before
- Distorts our sense of reality
- Makes us more dependent on machines than people

When such critiques incorporate comparisons to a previous time period when computers did not exist in large numbers (or at all), typically these critiques evoke nostalgia as a rhetorical act. These critiques want to persuade us that technology is bad because it replaces a better, previous situation. Critical comparisons between changes in the present and "better" times in the past are often nostalgic in design.

Kerouac's approach to nostalgia includes how he uses the past as a form of critique. A memory of a brother who died as a young boy, Kerouac's *Visions of Gerard* utilizes nostalgic references to tell its story. The novel's main character, Jean Duluoz, employs memories as narrative. The memory process itself creates a nostalgic experience; we tend to reorganize past experiences differently than the way they occurred in order to satisfy internal desires of longing. Nostalgia, then, depends on how the past becomes interpreted.

In order to make nostalgia the focus of his work, Kerouac isolates various cultural markers from specific temporal moments that will encourage emotional response. For instance, the narrative more than once refers to

- Old-time summer baseball games
- 1930s radios (and radio shows)
- 1930s fashion

Thus, it positions the 1930s as ideal. In particular, it contrasts a supposed 1930s moment of innocence with the early 1960s (the time when the novel is published).

In nostalgic writing, items we typically think of as mundane and unimportant become suddenly essential. Details take on unprecedented importance. Kerouac's fiction often begins with a minor detail—a counter top, the shape of a hamburger, the smell of gasoline—and uses the detail as a place to embark on a completely different discussion. In this sense, details function like myths. Out of the most mundane moment, an entire story evolves.

Nostalgic writing is most effective when it creates a longing in its audience. If the audience finds itself wanting to sit in an old diner, listen to a 1930s radio program, or drive a car that hasn't been manufactured in almost eighty years, then nostalgia takes place.

Let's update Kerouac's usage of nostalgia with a contemporary television advertisement. "The Harlem Years: 1975," a 2002 Nike commercial starring Toronto Raptors guard Vince Carter, exemplifies Kerouac's rhetorical usage of nostalgia in an electronic medium, television. Using 1975 as the focus of the commercial, Nike recreates what basketball fans often consider the NBA's Golden Years. The entire commercial looks as if it takes place in a 1970s New York City playground. Such games have become legendary in basketball lore because of the acrobatic moves playground players like Pee Wee Kirkland and Joe Hammond made in Rucker Park, Harlem, most of which never were performed in the NBA.

What are the rhetorical applications of nostalgia in the commercial? We recognize the setting as the 1970s because the crowd, who has gathered around the basketball court, sports large Afros and wears clothing styles typical of the seventies. Moreover, the players participating in the pick-up basketball game are dressed like 1970s basketball players; they too have Afros as well as knee-high socks and short-shorts. The only one who does not look like he belongs in the 1970s is Vince Carter, who is dressed in contemporary clothes and wearing the latest Nike shoes, the Nike Shox VC. By placing a considerable amount of 1970s iconography around Carter, however, the commercial suggests that wearing these shoes will make one play and feel like 1970s basketball players or as if one is in a 1970s basketball game. The Nike commercial, therefore, uses cool writing to evoke nostalgia for purposes of making a point regarding its product. At the end of this chapter, you will find an exercise that asks you to use nostalgia in a similar way when you write for the Web.

Popular culture nostalgia tends to come in waves of twenty years.

In the 1970s, nostalgia for the 1950s arose in television shows like *Happy Days* and *Laverne and Shirley.*

In the 1980s, *The Wonder Years* and *China Beach* recreated the 1960s.

In the 1990s, *That '70s Show* appeared.

And in 2002, *That '80s Show* debuted.

Think about how such patterns continue in other popular culture forms like music, fashion, or film. What kinds of nostalgic longings can you identify?

In what we might describe as a nostalgic Web surfing experience, you can see some of Nike's Web site for "The Harlem Years: 1975" by viewing the cached version saved at http://web.archive. org/web/20020306051313/, http://www. nike.com/nikebasketball/thefunk/index.jhtml, and http://web.archive.org/web/20020605020920/http://www.nike.com/nikebasketball/thefunk/index.jht ml. Nike has since taken the original site down, but The WayBack Machine Internet Archive saves sites on a regular basis for our nostalgic viewing.

William S. Burroughs

Burroughs' work addresses the influence of media and government on culture. Burroughs is especially concerned with how individuals can counter the oppressive nature of an highly influential media culture that dictates to its citizens what clothes to wear, what food to eat, where to live, how to behave, and how to think. For Burroughs, such control is mediated through writing. Television, film, political speeches, advertising, novels, and newspapers are all examples of writing we engage with on a daily basis. How these forms of writing are rhetorically constructed (i.e., how they use language and imagery) affects us in complex ways. What specifically frightened Burroughs is the way certain groups, like advertisers, subtly control thinking so that we are not aware of being controlled. Burroughs referred to these forms of subtle control as "media viruses," infections of society by controlling interests.

How, then, do we counter such control? Through writing, Burroughs contends. Writing is a powerful act that can be used against those who attempt to dominant our lives. Even more so, the writing used against us can be turned back on itself. In other words, writers can use the very pieces of writing being employed to control others. We've seen similar ideas when we studied the cultural jammers in Chapter 5. One method Burroughs proposes as a counter strategy is *the cut-up.*

The cut-up involves taking a piece of writing, cutting it into at least four sections, then rearranging the sections in new ways. Reading over the new arrangement produces alternative perspectives on the previous work. Cut-ups can reveal unspoken ideas, and they act as a resistance to the text's original meaning and purpose. If, for example, a political speech encourages citizens to discriminate against others, that speech can be cut up, rearranged, and made to say something entirely different, such as an argument for racial tolerance. The idea behind the cut-up is that when we experiment with language, we can produce alternative positions through association. Language is not a natural occurrence, but a construction put to work for various objectives. Moreover, words placed next to other words in a random way can create coherent prose.

To test Burroughs' ideas, we can practice doing the cut-up:

Take a newspaper. Cut up an article. Rearrange your cut-up sections so that the article says something new.

Do the same thing to a political speech or a text-based advertisement.

What do you come up with? Do you make the original text say something different?

Turn on your TV. Watch several commercials. Take notes on when images in these commercials switch abruptly, as if spliced with new, unrelated images. Is this a cut-up?

In the early 1960s, Burroughs' ideas challenged traditional notions regarding textual construction. When we write, do we progress in linear, rational manners? Or do we assemble a variety of ideas and concepts, mentally reconstruct them in various orders, and present them, sometimes in irrational ways? Actually, we perform cut-ups all the time, often without realizing we are doing so. Most of us compose at a computer. All word processing programs (such as Word or WordPerfect) allow us to cut and paste text in any order we choose. I can cut a line from one sentence and paste it onto another sentence. In addition, the desktop icons we use to cut up texts utilize the metaphor of scissors and glue to represent the ideas of cut and paste.

Normally, we don't pay much attention to this process. We take for granted that we can cut up texts, and we don't consider this accomplishment a very revolutionary act at all. Taking technology for granted, however, was the main point of Burroughs' work. Problems arise when we consider a media form, like the Web or an advertisement, as "natural" and "normal." We become desensitized to how these media forms affect us. We no longer think that *others'* writing affects how our lives are shaped. Instead, we view advertisements or speeches as innocent texts with no bearing on cultural behavior.

Being suspicious of how media is constructed does not equal becoming a conspiracy theorist. We can't spend all of our time searching for subliminal meanings in everything we read and watch. But being aware of textual construction does mean being critical of how meanings are created as well as what kind of ideologies and policies such images promote or play off of. Burroughs' argument has become important in our contemporary age of digital manipulation.

While Burroughs used the cut-up for critique, contemporary digital writers (advertisers, Web designers) often use it for noncritical practices. For example, pay attention to television commercials for sports utility vehicles (SUVs). Notice how the commercials often depict the automobiles as covering rugged terrain with little difficulty. The ads help us imagine driving these cars over mountain passes, through swamps, into difficult situations that a four-cylinder car couldn't handle. But are these cars actually driving through these areas? Or has technology been employed to cut and paste the image of the SUV into a mountain range? If we accept the image we see as natural, then we are duped into thinking this event took place. If we make ourselves aware of the power of cutting and pasting unrelated images and texts, we see how one can create persuasive discourse. These ads are persuasive. They present the SUV as an exceptional choice of transportation because of its extraordinary capabilities to handle difficult terrain. The challenge for cool writers is to reapply this strategy to creating critique rather than to selling products.

Car advertisements, in fact, demonstrate Burroughs' cut-up technique in very contemporary ways. For example, locate a car advertisement either online or in a print magazine. At http://www.adflip.com, you can find some examples like those discussed in this section. At http://www.adflip.com/images/ecards/ 13328.jpg, you will find an image for the Toyota MR2 Spider. What items have been cut up and pasted together to create this advertisement? The MR2 advertisement doesn't consist of a single image or text. Instead, we can identify the origins of its pieces and consider why Toyota placed those objects in the order it did. Why, for example, do you think that the image of the MR2 image is juxtaposed (that is, overlaid) with the blueprint image of the automobile? Examine the overlap of the two sections, the left and the right. Why is the page laid out in this manner? Take a careful look at the way Toyota uses words in this ad. Is there a logic to their placement on the right-hand side? Where is the emphasis, with the text or with the images? At http://www.adflip.com/images/ecards/12525.jpg, you can find another advertisement for the Acura MDX. How are images cut and pasted in this ad? How is text pasted? Why the juxtaposition of surfer and automobile? These are separate images taken at different times. In the ad, they are brought together for a specific rhetorical effect, to make the reader forge an association between the two. We need to consider the rhetorical effect of creating messages like these.

Now let's examine the cut-up rhetoric of a Web page. Go online to CNN's Web site at http://www.cnn.com.

Web sites like CNN's have become the norm for commercial Web sites. CNN's construction, however, does not reflect a "normal" process for assembling and presenting information. When we look at a Web page like this one, we notice a variety of texts and images put together as if this is one single text. This assemblage has its own rhetoric; that is, it's constructed in a very specific way in order to get a point across. To understand the rhetoric of a Web site like CNN's, we need to isolate several questions regarding its make up.

- How many disparate items can you locate on this one Web page?
- How has CNN cut up a variety of texts (the various stories and their respective headlines) and images, placing them in relationship to one another? What kind of method is employed here?

- Notice the advertisement or the Netscape symbols at the top of the site. Are they part of the text? Why or why not?
- What happens when you read the various headlines as if they belong to the same story (not an implausible action—imagine the experience the first readers of newspapers must have had when they read a variety of ideas put together on one page as if they all belonged together)?

Sites similar to CNN's find order in what should normally be a confusing placement of information. Consider your own experiences as a writer. How often do you struggle over how to organize your information? Do you wonder what might happen if you placed a section of your essay in one place rather than the other? Would the result be confusion or would you create an alternative approach to your topic? Have you ever been instructed to reorder your work in ways you felt were counter to your original intent? What effect did the new order have on your writing?

- Print out a Web site with a newspaper-like structure similar to CNN. Espn.com, Rapstation.com, ABC.com, and a number of other Web sites maintain a similar structure.
- Make a list of how many different items you see arranged on the page. This includes text and image. Which items normally wouldn't be associated with one another, but on the Web site are?
- Cut up the arrangement of the site. Rearrange it in a new order. What changes? How? How do your decisions contrast with those of the Web site designers?

Juxtaposition

As you may have noticed, cutting up text and images and rearranging their order involves juxtaposition. Juxtaposition means placing items together, often including items that normally have little to do with one another. In cool writing, juxtaposition specifically refers to the practices taught by people like William S. Burroughs who placed *unlike* text and images together. Why do this? What are the rhetorical effects of juxtaposition?

- Typically, we expect a "natural" order to how ideas are arranged.
- Juxtaposing unlike items challenges our expectations by forming unexpected possibilities.
- Such challenges often provoke us into considering new ideas and positions on subjects we've grown accustomed to and familiar with.
- Juxtaposition, therefore, rhetorically allows us to create new ideas and get us thinking about the familiar in alternative ways. Familiarity can limit our ability to think differently about a given issue. When we make a given image or idea unfamiliar, we open up new possibilities for meaning making.

- Alternative positions often allow us to innovate on previous ideas as well as to invent completely new concepts.
- Juxtaposition gives us a new way to write about a given idea.

When Burroughs teaches us how to use the cut-up, he's making a case for the process known as juxtaposition. Burroughs felt that juxtaposition defamiliarizes images, language, relationships, and roles that we take for granted. In fact, juxtaposing unlike images and texts is in itself a fairly familiar process, only we don't usually consider it as such. We've already mentioned how word processing can juxtapose different drafts or ideas on one screen, but we can also think of how media in general adopts this practice. When you watch a movie, for example, what you're seeing isn't a continuous narrative taking place in real time. Instead, you're watching several different moments, each shot at different times and out of order, reconstructed and spliced together. The various shots become juxtaposed so that a new image emerges—the film you are viewing. If you looked at the various scenes in the order they were shot, you would get a completely different impression of the movie and what it was about. But you believe that the natural order of the film is what is represented to you on the screen.

Spend time examining the ways advertisements and Web sites are constructed. Look at how the creators of these media forms juxtapose unlike items to create new products.

Watch the films of Soviet filmmaker Sergei Eisenstein. Working in the 1920s, Eisenstein wanted to teach uneducated Russians about Marxism. He opted to employ juxtaposition in his films as a teaching method. By bringing together various disparate items, Eisenstein felt he could recreate visually the Marxist lessons he wanted to teach.

Watch films like *October* and *Potemkin*. Do some additional research on Eisenstein's concept of "intellectual montage," the particular practice of juxtaposition he created.

Why do you think images are so effective as teaching tools? Why would uneducated people react strongly to images over words? Can you imagine a project in which you would only use images to teach a lesson to an audience?

Burroughs' interest in the juxtaposition of media forms for argumentative purposes concentrates heavily on this point of contention, the widespread belief that representations maintain a natural existence. Often we deem media representations as natural when, in fact, they are carefully constructed in order to elicit a specific reaction from an audience. In this way, representations control our responses, but they do so in ways that leave us believing we are free to make our own decisions and choices. Burroughs' work destabilizes control by attempting to wrestle it away from controlling interests. By rearranging corporate and governmental language in provocative ways, Burroughs felt *he* was gaining control over how audiences are exposed to messages.

Burroughs' novel *Nova Express*, for instance, opens with a series of juxtapositions that simultaneously present a dire warning of contemporary corporate influence as well as critique such influence by bringing together unlike textual citations. The novel's first page presents a series of quotations, all saying different things at once. Juxtaposed with these quotations is Burroughs' own proclamation that control will soon be reapplied to new forces.

Calling on the "boards syndicates and governments of the earth" to beware of developing attempts to counter their influence, the novel's first page declares, "For God's sake don't let that Coca-Cola thing out." In line with what we have been discussing so far, we can see Burroughs' comment as a reflection on how we absorb media messages without distinction or critique. "Don't let that Coca-Cola thing out" uses the image of the popular soft drink as an iconic representation of commercial industry. Burroughs pleads for corporate influence to be contained, and its power prevented from taking over popular expression. In other words, if we "let that Coca-Cola thing out," we succumb to corporate control over language, and, in the end, behavior.

- Let's consider Coca-Cola as a test case for an extensive commercial practice. How often do you see, for example, Coca-Cola images in media forms? Do some research. Look for as many Coca-Cola references you can find in movies, TV shows, songs, comic strips, speeches, billboards, newspaper supplements and articles, print advertisements, sporting events, products, etc.
- For example, do you find toys or products that carry the Coca-Cola label? If so, is this a toy or an advertisement? Which? And does it matter that a child may play with a toy truck that says Coca-Cola on it? Will exposure to Coca-Cola encourage the child (or one of us) to eventually buy the soft drink?
- Does Coca-Cola exemplify the problems Burroughs feared? Does it represent the complex relations commercial enterprises maintain within our daily lives? How do we deal with the overabundance of corporate symbols in our lives? Is it a problem or is it acceptable? Can we contain the "Coca-Cola thing" or are we doomed to its media dominance? Think back to Chapter 5's discussion of Adbusters and The Billboard Liberation Front.

Juxtaposed with *Nova Express'* Coca-Cola image are other quotes that either contrast or complement the image. Indeed, throughout the novel, Burroughs cuts and pastes from newspapers, television speeches, his own writings, and literary works like T.S. Eliot's *The Wasteland*, Franz Kafka's *The Trial*, and William Shakespeare's *The Tempest*. As readers, we are never sure what is a quotation or what is Burroughs' writing. We can think of his work as an early example of digital sampling; Burroughs mixes various texts to create one piece of writing, much in the way digital samplers mix music.

One of the novel's major characters, The Subliminal Kid, captures the process of juxtaposition through his behavior. Burroughs informs his readers that The Subliminal Kid sets up tape recorders and transmitters in various bars and cafés. Afterwards, The Subliminal Kid remixes his recordings and plays them back in juxtaposition with one another and in a different order. The effect becomes disorienting and yet persuasive in the way it constructs new arguments about contemporary issues. Even more compelling is how The Subliminal Kid's experiment feeds off of everyday language, the ways it uses everyday conversation to comment on what is occurring politically and socially. Burroughs believed that mere exposure to a variety of voices, sounds, and ideas influences people to invent and innovate. Listening to The Subliminal Kid's mixes of voices talking at once, therefore, sparks the thinking process. But so would walking down the street and taking note of isolated conversations, overhead announcements, and street noise.

Test The Subliminal Kid's tape recording experiments.

Go to a bar, restaurant, café, shopping mall, busy street, or favorite hangout on campus. Record or take detailed notes on the conversations you hear.

Later, when you have accumulated enough material, use your recordings or notes to create a piece of writing. Don't include any of your words. Create your ideas out of the ideas of others. One way to do this is to cut up your notes and rearrange them in a new order. Or you can transcribe your recordings, cut them up, and rearrange them as well.

Present your work as an academic paper for your English course.

Recommended Reading

Burroughs, William S. *Naked Lunch*. New York: Grove Press, 1982 (1959).
———. *Nova Express*. New York: Grove Press, 1992 (1964).
———. *The Ticket That Exploded*. New York: Grove Weidenfeld, 1987 (1964).
Corso, Gregory. *Bomb*. San Francisco: City Lights Books, 1958.
Ferlinghetti, Lawrence. *A Coney Island of the Mind*. New York: W.W. Norton & Company, 1974.
Ginsberg, Allen. *Howl and other Poems*. San Francisco, City Lights Books, 1959.
———. *Planet News: 1961–1967*. San Francisco: City Lights Books, 1968.
———. *Reality Sandwiches*. San Francisco, CA: City Lights Books, 1963.
Kerouac, Jack. *The Subterraneans*. New York: Grove, 1958.
———. *On the Road*. New York: Signet, 1957.
———. *Visions of Cody*. New York: McGraw-Hill, 1970.
———. *Visions of Gerard*. New York: Farrar, Straus and Company, 1963.
Plimpton, George, ed. *Beat Writers at Work*. New York: Modern Library, 1999.
Snyder, Gary. *Turtle Island*. New York: New Directions, 1974.

Recommended Viewing

The Source. A documentary on the Beats.
Towers Open Fire. Dir. Anthony Balch and William S. Burroughs. Myotic Fire Video, 1990.
MTV's *Biorhythm*. While no longer on the air, this biography series presents many of the rhetorical ideas discussed in this chapter. In this series, MTV used

collage and cut and pasted clips, headings, and sound to present a biography on a celebrity.

VH1's *Behind the Music*. Nostalgic documentaries of rock bands who rose to the top and eventually fell from grace.

VH1's *Pop Up Videos*. These videos take previously broadcast videos and juxtapose new, often witty, commentary.

Music videos in general. Note how most videos incorporate both nostalgic elements and juxtaposition in order to deliver a message.

Web Site

On the Web site for this book, you'll find links and information regarding HTML which will be useful for completing the "How to Be a Beat Web Designer" assignment below. You'll also find further information on the Beats and the cut-up process.

Class Discussion

1. Even in our media-intensive culture, it can be difficult to grasp and even accept Burroughs' idea of the cut-up. Some students find it silly; others find it challenging. In particular, because many English classes emphasize novels and poems as exemplary works of art, we may find it disturbing to cut them up. And because many writing classes emphasize authorial purpose, we might be reluctant to destroy that purpose by rearranging the writer's words.

   As a class, debate the effectiveness of the cut-up. Draw from contemporary examples of cut-ups so that the discussion is concrete and supported.

2. A popular media form that uses juxtaposition extensively is the comic book. As a class, bring in comic books and explore how comic books juxtapose image and text as well as how they juxtapose the various panels. What is the rhetoric of comic book juxtapositions?

3. Does Kerouac's usage of nostalgia appear in hip-hop as well? How does hip-hop's sampling resemble Kerouac's nostalgia? Discuss how hip-hop songs sometimes are nostalgic for specific fashions, TV shows, popular trends, or other songs.

4. When you save images off of the Web to use on your home page or in a Web project, are your motives for doing so ever influenced by nostalgia? In other words, do you choose images because they are from a specific time period (the 1980s or 1990s) or because they remind you of a moment in your past?

Exercises

1. *The Nostalgia Assignment*. Kerouac uses nostalgia in order to critique technologically changed living conditions. His nostalgia depends on using cultural icons from the past and recontextualizing them in new ways.

   Create a site that uses images and text from a specific moment in the past (the 1970s, the 1930s, the 1850s, etc.) to make a statement about a contemporary issue. Within the selected time period, focus on film, advertising, political speeches and issues, comics, television, sports, science, etc. in order to accumulate material. Your site should stick to one temporal period in order to reflect its nostalgic style.

2. *How to Be a Beat Web Designer*. Much of what the Beats teach is relevant to Web design. Their interest in nonlinearity and cut-ups shares similar attributes with Web designers' interest in constructing Web sites. For this assignment, we'll push the notion that the Beats are relevant to electronic writing by using their work as instructions for how to be a Web designer. This assignment requires additional readings. We've provided a short list of relevant Beat writings in the Recommended Readings list, but more exist.

Do an inventory of various Beat novels, poems, and interviews. Make a list of every point about writing made or performed by these writers. You want to note how they write as well as what they say about writing. For example, when reading Kerouac's *The Subterraneans*, you will see that he uses nonlinearity to construct the narrative. Nonlinearity, therefore, will be a point to mark down on your list. In Burroughs' work, the cut-up is another point to mark down. There are many more we can come up with.

After you have accumulated a significant number of ideas regarding writing, construct a guide that explains how to use these ideas in order to create Web pages. Only, instead of writing a descriptive step-by-step account of each point, perform each item while explaining it.

For example, if you choose to include nonlinearity, then your section on that point should be nonlinear. Or if you want to include in your guide the cut-up, then that section should be cut up or maybe even involve readers in cutting up the text and reassembling it.

Use the various scripts and HTML codes we've used previously to make your case as compelling as possible. Experiment with refresh tags, drag-and-drop scripts, tables, etc. Visit this book's Web site for further information regarding where to find such codes.

Chapter

12

Technology

This chapter and the following chapters emphasize the role of technology in cool writing. What, though, do we mean by technology? Do we mean any machine or motorized system? Do we mean scientific achievements? Do we mean communication-based technologies, i.e., information technologies? Even if we narrow our definition to information technologies, what do we include within such a broad framework? Do we include any device used to distribute or store information? Cell phones, pagers, Web sites, satellites, television, and radio all might be situated within such a definition. These devices alter information storage, reception, and delivery.

For instance, one popular commercial for a Nokia cell phone shows two teenagers at a party who have difficulty communicating over loud music. Finally, the male teenager types a message into his cell phone; the text instantly appears on the female's phone. "Good cheese," it reads. Even though they are next to one another, they rely on information technology to communicate. A machine replaces speech. The commercial identifies the influential role technology plays in communication even though it poses such a role as ideal. In this final part of our look at cool, we'll question such assumptions and attempt to look at the larger implications of technologically oriented communication systems.

If we stick with the limited definition of technology as information technology, however, in addition to computer-based devices, we also need to consider the pencil, the pen, the eraser, and the blackboard. All of these devices are technologies. These inventions, which we have come to forget about because of their ubiquitous and accepted nature, changed information distribution as much as cell phones have today. They also altered individual writing performance. The pencil and eraser, for instance, limited the problem of making a mistake. The introduction of the eraser into everyday writing practices diminished the permanent nature of writing. With pencils and erasers, writing mistakes could be quickly eradicated at little cost or trouble. The eraser gave writing a more flexible status in communicative practices.

The computer belongs to this technological tradition. And with the mass distribution of the personal computer came a number of specific writing applications that we are beginning to feel comfortable working with (just as we are now comfortable using an eraser): word processing, spreadsheets, e-mail, and even hypertext. Hypertext was introduced in 1992, and for most of us its novelty has since dissipated. Every new computer comes with a hypertext editor for making Web pages (Notepad), and more advanced editors that insert the HTML code for users are easily available and affordable. In addition, word processing programs like Word or WordPerfect often come with applications that convert text to HTML.

When we surf the Web, most of the time we pay little attention to how sites are constructed. We see images, texts, and hyperlinks, but unless curiosity strikes, we don't uncover the technology that creates these items. As we've already briefly seen, technological expression has a rhetoric. This, in turn, includes all forms of expression because we can't spread our ideas without technology. Writing is itself a technology. To be effective writers, however, we need to figure out how to use technology to make ourselves understood.

As a class, take an informal survey about what each class member feels constitutes technology. Write a definition explaining what technology is, does, and performs. In addition to composing a definition, have each member write down specific examples that demonstrate the definitions.

How different are your responses? Where are they similar? What does this say about our notion of technology?

This textbook's main focus is, after all, to think about a rhetoric for electronic writing; that is, specifically, we want to use cool as a tool for constructing meaning while engaging with electronic writing formats like hypertext. Our initial introduction to cool came via technology (the Web sites that use cool to list out of the ordinary places to visit on the Web), but we haven't, for the most part, explored cool writing in relationship to technology. We've offered a number of ways other media forms (music, literature, and advertising) can be used to write electronically, but not how the electronic medium uses cool. Therefore, in this chapter and the next, we turn to actual electronic practices in order to see how cool as electronic writing works.

Electronic Writing

The expression "electronic writing" is itself a loosely defined term. Electronic writing can mean anything from making a home page to using PowerPoint to word processing to working with complex computer codes. Thomas Edison once conceived the idea of an electric pen; more recently, a two-page print advertisement for Intel, entitled "Go Digital," describes how computers equipped with its processor allow electronic writers to edit, crop, retouch, mix, burn, groove, compose, and jam. Often, when we hear the expression electronic writing, we think of the World Wide Web and hypertext. At the very least, we imagine using a computer to compose texts. In order to grasp the rhetorical possibilities we can draw upon when we use computers to write, we need to query our relationship to electronic writing. Why is electronic writing different from print? What role do computers today play when we write? How have they changed our understanding of what it means to write?

While thinking about these questions, consider the types of exercises each chapter has asked you to do. Are these the kinds of writing assignments you would typically do in a writing class? Why or why not? How do the assignments in this book (all designed for cool writing) differ from print-based writing assignments?

These questions are the subjects of long debates on the merits of computers and writing. In the early 1980s, controversy erupted over the integration of computers into writing classrooms; many educators feared students would become too dependent on the spell-checking function, or would favor the machine over the writing process itself. These educators felt computers might displace the human interaction that typically occurs in a classroom. They also feared students would lose personal involvement in writing, a belief that assumes we are more connected to our writing when we use a pen or pencil, as opposed to a computer (these debates still exist regarding distance education). It no longer makes sense, however, to debate whether or not computers should be used to write. They *are* being used for writing all the time, in various ways.

Most of us feel comfortable sitting at a computer and using a word processing program to write a letter, an essay, a resume, or some other document. Word processing provides a good example of how public doubt regarding technology's effectiveness eventually transformed into a mainstream and familiar practice. We no longer think twice about turning on a word processing program to compose a document. Today, word processing seems familiar because:

- We've grown used to it over the last twenty years.
- The previous technology for word processing, the typewriter, no longer exists in large numbers.
- It draws upon the typewriter, a familiar technology of past composing practices. Finished text on an electronic typewriter and finished text on a word processor look very similar. For this reason, most people accept word processing as a suitable substitute for the typewriter. Word processing didn't eliminate the familiar typewriter interface or structure; it merely added new elements on to the previous tool.
- It worked with, not against, other electronic writing practices. The cut-and-paste function of word processing parallels similar methods present in film and television production, advertising, and musical recording.

Word processing, therefore, has made a fairly smooth transition into acceptance as a form of electronic writing. The change from one writing medium to another, then, is easiest when the new medium exists in large numbers, the old medium fades out and isn't abruptly replaced, and the new medium doesn't radically alter the old. What happens when these conditions are not met, but we want to use technology for other types of writing? How do we typically respond? Do we immediately embrace an alternative usage of technology for communicative purposes, or do we fear its inclusion in our daily practice?

Technological innovations often build off of familiar ideas or interfaces. Open up your word processing program. Look at how the program displays symbols and instructions for the various tasks it can perform. How many of the symbols and instructions are familiar and easy to recognize? When you see the symbol of a scissors, do you immediately know what it does? When you see the magnifying glass positioned over a piece of paper, do you know what it will do without consulting the help guide?

How many computer programs do you know of that use very similar interfaces and toolbars? What about the images on your desktop? Trashcans, filing cabinets, pens: what do these symbols mean? Why are these icons (and not others) used to describe the programs which they will open for you when you click them?

Difficult questions emerge when we attempt to introduce into our common vocabulary other forms of electronic writing, like hypertext. Unlike the smooth transition from the typewriter to the word processor, hypertext introduces a number of unfamiliar elements to writing: links, tags and codes, tables, and images. In addition, as many assignments in this book have asked us to consider, other coded languages like DHTML and JavaScript can be incorporated into hypertext with minimal difficulty if others write the codes and make them publicly available for cutting and pasting. You'll find examples of such codes on this book's Web site.

We'll discuss hypertext in more detail in the next chapter. For now, we want to expand our conception of electronic writing much in the way hypertext has expanded word processing. Hypertext borrows the traditional alphabetic writing we do in word processing, but it also adds tactics to manipulate the language we're accustomed to using. Our first step towards examining electronic writing is to look at other practices that turn the familiar into something new and, at first, unfamiliar. We'll begin this process by returning to a familiar subject we've already discussed, hip-hop. We'll examine another form of electronic writing prevalent in hip-hop, skratching, and we'll progressively work our way towards a discussion of another form of electronic writing, hypertext.

 Come up with three to five examples of writing forms you would classify as electronic writing. Why do you consider these writing forms "electronic?" What do they have in common? Where are they different?

Have you ever been asked to use one of these forms for a school writing assignment? Why or why not?

Try to imagine the first time a student was required to turn in an assignment written on a *typewriter* and not by hand. What might the teacher and/or the student have said in response to this technology-driven demand?

Hip-Hop

In this section, we'll return to hip-hop culture and examine its interest in another version of electronic writing, skratching. Since its inception, hip-hop has maintained strong links to technology. As we discussed earlier in this book, because hip-hop's early DJs often came from impoverished neighborhoods and had little expendable income, they worked without expensive equipment and could not afford costly hours at major recording studios. Many of these DJs had received some form of education at technical schools in New York City, so they had good knowledge of how electronics function. Without modern equipment, they managed to construct their own systems from old parts and used turntables. In fact, early DJs worked from a "use whatever you can find" methodology. Whatever bits and pieces they could assemble together worked.

Without mobile sources of electricity for their sound systems, for instance, many DJs would plug directly into public park street lights. Without enough money to buy new records to spin at parties, DJs built collections out of bargain street sales, often accumulating large numbers of out-of-print recordings or records by obscure bands. These unknown records formed the backbone of early hip-hop music. Instead of playing these records in their entirety, DJs like Kool Herc, Afrika Bambaataa, and Grandmaster Flash discovered in turntable technology a new way to play records. By concentrating on one section of the record's groove and by mixing this section with a groove on another disc, they could create music out of various prerecorded sounds. Mixers and turntables, neither in itself a technology new to music, became instruments for composing. Thus, hip-hop's origins are in innovative applications of old technology:

- Unused electrical outlets often located on street lights
- Old records bought at discount prices (used "writing" that audiences weren't familiar with or had lost interest in)
- Mixers used for fading sound in and out
- Turntables used for playing records

Record playing became the basis of a new compositional form. Since we've already highlighted sampling, in this chapter we'll focus on how hip-hop innovated record usage and led to what many DJs call a new form of literacy: skratching. Skratching has played a major role in rethinking how technology shapes expression. It proposes that writing can take place in alternative venues, and that those who are capable of writing in these areas create an alternative form of expression. DJs who practice skratching claim a new language and, therefore, a new literacy. Our task is to generalize the lesson of skratching to our own writing and understandings of literacy. What does skratching teach us about producing ideas in new media environments like the World Wide Web? We'll explore this question more fully as we examine skratching as a rhetorical practice.

Literacy

Before we discuss skratching, we need to make a slight digression and consider the larger issue of literacy. When we discuss literacy, we normally enter into a conversation regarding the ability to read and write. In American culture, learning these skills promotes one as an educated person with high values and civic responsibility. As the American philosopher Henry David Thoreau wrote in *Walden*, "To read well, that is to read true books in a true spirit, is a noble exercise, and one that will task the reader more than any exercise which the customs of the day esteem." When public figures claim a "literacy crisis," they are usually referring to what they perceive as a widespread inability to read and write at basic levels. Literacy, however, means more than just reading and writing. It involves an understanding of how to use language in order to construct meaning. Writing without meaning isn't anything more than typed words on a page. For instance, if we use the word cool without understanding its meanings or even applying its meanings (as the book teaches you to do), we aren't using the word in a literate manner.

When we interject technology into the picture, we need to address how technology shapes literacy. The two forces are always intertwined. New innovations in technology have direct effects on literacy practices. For example, before the invention of the printing press in the 1500s, few people knew how to read and write, and, consequently, the ability to produce written texts was a limited activity. Those who could read and write typically belonged to the aristocracy or the clergy. In turn, information distribution and creation came only from those with power. Literacy was a restricted practice. For those who couldn't participate in this practice (the poor, the working class, women), literacy was determined by their ability to memorize and recite information heard in public speeches or in local marketplaces. Therefore, learning occurred in sizeable gatherings in public locations.

When the printing press made texts available to a large number of people at once, eventually the demand for widespread literacy grew. Consequently, as larger concentrations of people learned to read and write, these activities began to take place in solitary places like one's own home. One no longer needed to be in a public location to receive information. One could now read a book alone, think about what one had read, and even reread the book in order to understand its content better. When individuals felt the need to express themselves, they, too, could do so in private, at a personal desk or some related writing space. The printed book altered notions of literacy.

> Some questions to consider as you absorb the information in this chapter regarding literacy:
>
> What is a codex?
>
> What is a manuscript?
>
> What did these pre-printing press items look like?
>
> They were once the cornerstones for spreading literacy. Today, popular culture forms seem to have a significant impact on how information is created and distributed. Research these items online and then compare them with three contemporary items (like a music sharing program, TV, an MP3 player, a DVD player, etc). What are the differences? What are the similarities? How do new media change our understandings of communication?

Today we can think of new developments in technology and communication as having similar effects on people. Computers shape communication in a number of ways and form new understandings of what literacy entails. When we hear someone mention "computer literacy," implied in this phrase is the idea of an individual capable of turning on a computer and successfully using its software. But computer literacy, as this textbook continuously stresses, also means producing knowledge with computers, knowing how to create discourse with computers, and rhetorically being persuasive with computers. There is a big difference between being able to turn a computer on and knowing how to make meaning with computer applications.

Hip-hop's immediate attraction to computer technology makes it an excellent place to consider how one version of computer literacy unfolds. Digital samplers and some turntables have computer chips that allow the machines to record and save music, manipulate sound, and play back compositions in a variety of styles. Turntable stylists, those who spin records, often see their usage of these machines as a step towards creating a new form of electronic literacy. These stylists spin records in complex ways called skratching. Skratching involves the extension of a record's rhythms and beats by carefully moving the record back and forth as well as by spinning it in short bursts. Those who practice this act "skratch" the record's grooves. The squeaking noise that emerges becomes manipulated to form a new sound. The musicians who practice skratching are often known as turntablists.

Why should we examine turntablists spinning records in a writing class? Aren't the two areas of communication completely different and unrelated? Shouldn't our focus be solely on writing? What does playing records have to do with learning to write?

To think through these questions, we have to consider what we mean by writing and by literacy. We also have to decide if we are open to learning about alternative writing practices in order to understand how contemporary writing differs from more traditional methods of expression, like jotting one's ideas down on paper. This doesn't mean that we reject communicating by writing alphabetic words on paper. On the contrary, we most likely will always employ the alphabet as a means for self-expression. But we also want to explore additional writing possibilities so that, at the very least, we gain better command over how the traditional fares against technological innovations in communication. What new rhetorical possibilities do new media forms (like the turntable or the computer) offer us? Even if we don't opt for spinning records, which is not what this chapter recommends anyway, we can learn methods from other computer-based writing systems that are applicable to electronic writing.

Turntablism provides students of electronic writing (which we all are) with a model for how to create meaning with new technology. The question of who is or isn't "literate" is also the question that asks how well we use technology to produce knowledge. Including turntablism in this discussion adds a dimension we probably haven't considered yet. The purpose isn't to become a turntablist or to spin records in the classroom, but rather to study how this specific form of electronic writing works so that we may apply its approach to our own work. Because turntablism is based on an object, the turntable, we can consider how objects of communication influence communication itself.

To begin with, skratching is analogous to the typewriter/word processor example we mentioned previously. Turntablists take an old technology, the record player, and rather than abandon it completely for new technology, they refashion it with computer parts. The new product blends both the old and the new. In the computer writing classroom, we take the old forms of writing (developing a claim, establishing supports, organizing our work in coherent ways, proofreading for mechanics) and we reshape this process to accommodate technological changes. All along, we have asked you to think about these changes in relationship to cool. The various rhetorical strategies we've extracted from the Web, advertising, and literature demonstrate these additions. As we examine how turntablists construct sound, you'll no doubt see similarities to some of the other forms of cool writing we've explored.

Skratchadelia

Popular culture has shown increasing interest in skratching. Once a marginal activity, skratching has since acquired mainstream acceptance. Notably, like the earlier examples of cool and business we explored, skratching has attracted large corporations who use the practice in their commercials as a way to lure young customers to their products. Burger King, for instance, has run a commercial featuring skratching pioneer DJ Skribble. In a Gap Denim commercial, two male DJs skratch a funky tune while a woman dances between them. At the commercial's end, she turns to the camera and says, "My first love? Boys who skratch." Wintergreen gum's commercial, a cartoon of a supermarket, features a checkout girl running a pack of gum over the electronic scanner. As she does so, she skratches the gum, producing music. The commercial ends with the slogan "Even cooler, even better." The commercial forges a connection between cool, consumerism (grocery shopping), and skratching. By tapping into these areas simultaneously, Wintergreen suggests a strong connection to its viewers, a connection we can also use as we think of skratching as another version of cool writing. On *Writing About Cool's* Web site, you can find links to images from these commercials.

What do these commercials do rhetorically that we have seen in other media displays? In order to answer the question, go back to previous chapters in this book and revisit some of the examples we discussed.

The process of skratching records often goes by the name of skratchadelia. The music theorist Kodwo Eshun calls skratchadelia "wreckage made rhythmic." What he means is that the initial confusing sounds that emerge from skratching eventually produce a rhythm. Skratchadelia begins, then, like most writing. We have a number of ideas we want to put down, but we aren't yet sure how to combine them so that they make sense to our readers; essentially, we suffer from internal writer noise. In the 1970s, educator Peter Elbow drew attention to this aspect of the writing process. Elbow felt that the way around such mental noise is to just jot down all your ideas at once. Later, you can sort through these initial, noisy writings for a coherent idea. Elbow called this process "freewriting." In hip-hop, the analogy to freewriting is skratching. In fact, hip-hop's *freestyle* method of rapping involves on-the-spot lyrical compositions that attempt to merge a number of instantaneous thoughts at once. Freestyle, like freewriting, attempts to make clear the various ideas that become entangled in our thought process. In music, like in writing, there exists an inordinate amount of material to learn from, play, and incorporate into a new composition. Therefore, an alternative strategy needed to be formed in order to make sense of all this material. Skratching addresses the need for another approach to composing.

Like other forms of hip-hop, skratching cuts and pastes previous recordings and sounds. Unlike hip-hop's sampling, skratching integrates the technology itself into this process. In other words, the tool one uses to write with becomes part of the writing itself. Imagine your pen or keyboard being as important to your writing's final outcome as the words you use. This is what skratching does with turntables. It integrates the tools of technology into the writing process. The idea is difficult to understand at first because we typically separate the tools for writing from the writing process. As computer technology plays a more significant role in writing, the two areas become intertwined. As we previous noted, we're already familiar with certain writing tools:

- Pen
- Pencil
- Eraser
- Word processor

Each of these tools generated a considerable amount of interest or controversy upon its introduction into mainstream usage because of the tool's unique characteristics. Skratching most likely won't ever make the turntable as mainstream as the pencil; but skratching might become more predominant in discursive exchange than it is today.

There are two important rhetorical acts in skratching: cuts and breaks. Cuts are the parts of a recording isolated and used again in an alternative way. Breaks are the moments in a recording when the rhythm emerges. When these brief moments of sound are captured in a computer's memory, they take the name of break. Breaks comprise a typical sampled recording. Kodwo Eshun writes, "The cut is a command, a technical and conceptual operation which cuts the lines of association." Eshun draws attention to how skratching cuts segmented sections of a song from the rest of the song. In other words, cuts break associative links in previous recordings.

Skratching's relevance to writing, then, also involves cutting associations. Too often, we construct arguments based on previous assumptions and associations without carefully interrogating these beliefs. We write as if our first thoughts, those based on our assumptions, are innately correct. However, assumptions and associations, as we outlined in this book's beginning, are culturally formed. They are not natural occurrences. We create these images based on our exposure to books, magazines, politics, movies, comics, conversations, religion, and other forms of expression. When we make problematic associations, like the angry black male example we discussed in Chapter 8, faulty arguments ensue. Other times, we make associations that may be logical, but are uninformed because of our cultural commitment to an immediate impression we've made. Often, these impressions depend on familiar positions we've come to accept as normal. In turn, we're hesitant to question how these ideas were formed or what kinds of meanings they may convey. The expressions are meant to generalize specific incidents as representative of universal behavior. Such generalizations, however, exclude the various cultural factors that make all of our experiences different.

One of the most obvious examples of this is the "self-made man" motif. In American culture, we tend to believe that if you just work hard and believe in yourself, you will achieve your objective. While the sentiment is encouraging, the assumption made here ignores other factors that play into how we succeed or don't succeed, issues we raised when we discussed Amiri Baraka's definition of cool in Chapter 6. Consider these influential factors the expression "self-made man" ignores:

- Racial, disability, or gender prejudices
- Economic disadvantages
- Political situations or oppression
- Lack of educational access
- Health issues

Many common expressions often pass without any critical examination. Self-made man is one example. What are some others? How might you begin to critically dissect these phrases?

The directive to cut associations, then, can serve a critical purpose. It can give us opportunity to rethink various cultural biases we've come to depend upon, or it can open up new possibilities by diminishing our dependence on the familiar. If, in your writing, you cut associations with the phrase "self-made man," you are performing a critical act by "skratching" that phrase. This book has repeatedly asked you to cut your associations to the familiar word cool. In place of the commonplace idea of cool as referring to an object or person of high esteem and value, we have studied cool as a form of writing. By cutting your past associations, you open yourself up to new readings. In a way, we are "skratching" the word cool! And following this line of thought, we are also skratching our previous conceptions of literacy:

- In print culture, literacy implies using the alphabet to understand meanings and produce new ideas.
- In electronic culture, literacy includes print's definitions, but adds the ways computer-based technologies like personal computers, various software programs, and digital sampling can extend the process of the construction of meaning.

The second point "cuts" our previous conceptions of what it means to be a functionally literate member of our culture, by "breaking" with a new definition. Skratching, therefore, performs a rhetorical act.

By cutting associations, engaging in critique, and producing alternative viewpoints, skratching shapes its own literate practice. All that is missing is a method for recording and reproducing ideas created by skratching. In other words, skratching needs a *writing* system capable of recording its ideas.

In the now-defunct online magazine *Feed*, Bruno Franklin's article "The DJs New Lexicon" described one DJ's attempt to create a notation system for skratching. Just as traditional music uses various notation symbols so that musicians can repeat performances, DJ Radar (Jason Grossfeld) created a writing system for skratching.

A notation system is as important as having an alphabet. We use the alphabet to form words, phrases, and sentences, all of which record our thoughts and ideas. Without an alphabet, our ideas would be momentary, or would last only as long as we could remember them. A notation system is based on the notion of repeatability; the ability to write out ideas and read them over and over keeps those ideas alive. Consequently, individuals must be trained to read the notation and write it out as well in order to learn from past thinking and in order to develop new thought. Therefore, when skratching enthusiasts like DJ Radar work to develop a method for recording their ideas, they are, in effect, inventing a form of literacy.

Skratching's overall importance to cool writing is in how it creates its own literate practice through innovations in computer technology. Documentation of how we write in computer environments is as important as the computer technology we use to write. In the song "Skratch Language," DJ Shortcut of the skratching group Invisibl Skratch Piklz states, "DJ Cube and DJ Dis are going to talk to us in Skratch Language." DJ shortcut suggests skratching is a language complementing the day-to-day language we have grown accustomed to using in the workplace, school, or home.

Where can we use skratching for communication? The most obvious place seems to be the generalized area we call popular culture (music belongs to popular culture). But if we are willing to take chances with our writing, if we are interested in adapting some rhetorical lessons from skratching for cool writing, then we should be able to apply skratching to other areas as well, including the classroom where we do a considerable amount of writing. If you skratch an idea for an English or history paper, for instance, you would be cutting certain assumptions that are typically assumed to be true. At the end of this chapter are exercises designed to get you to think about skratching and your own writing. As you work with the exercises, think about how you are applying a practice you might initially find alien to school (skratching) to your writing.

Further Reading

Brewster, Bill, and Frank Broughton. *Last Night a DJ Saved My Life. The History of the Disc Jockey*. New York: Grove Press, 2000.

Bruno, Franklin. "The DJs New Lexicon." *Feed Magazine* 5 May 2001. Originally published at: http://www.feedmagazine.com/templates/default.php3?a_id=1700. It can now be accessed through a cached version at: http://web.archive.org/web/20010604120103/, http://www.feedmagazine.com/templates/ default.php3?a_id=1700

Eshun, Kodwo. *More Brilliant than the Sun: Adventures in Sonic Fiction*. London: Quartet, 1999.

Poschardt, Ulf. *DJ Culture*. London: Quartet, 1998.

Wired, Electronic Music Issue, May 2002.

DJ Qbert's Web site: http://www.djqbert.com/

Electronic music magazine *Xlr8r's* Web site: http://www.xlr8r.com/

Recommended Viewing

Scratch. Dir. Doug Pray. Atlantic Video, 2002.

Recommended Listening

Various artists. *Return of the DJ* (several volumes exist). Bomb Hip Hop, 2003.

Invisbl Skratch Piklz. *Shiggar Fragger, Vols. 1–5*. Hip Hop Slam, 1998.

Mixmaster Mike. *Anti-Theft Device*. Asphodel Records, 1998.

———. *Spin Pyscle*. Moonshine Music, 2001.

Web Site

Visit *Writing About Cool's* Web site for more examples of digital sampling, skratching, and turntablism, as well as additional links to online resources.

Class Discussion

1. How did you initially react to the discussion of skratching? Does it belong in a writing textbook and classroom? Do you agree with the rationale we provide for including it? If not, why not?
2. Spend time as a class defining your previous conceptions of what literacy entails. How does this chapter challenge or sustain those ideas?
3. Does this chapter encourage you to think of cool as a form of literacy? Why or why not?
4. How does the major discipline that you are studying (history, accounting, chemistry) define its own sense of literacy? In other words, what tools does one need to produce knowledge and meaning in that discipline?
5. Your class might want to spend time listening to skratch records to get a better understanding of what the music is doing to traditional forms of musical production. In turn, you might think of how you, as a writer, can challenge traditional forms of writing.

Exercises

1. *Design Your Own Writing Practice.* While unfamiliarity of skratching may be a bit daunting for some of you at first, the overall relationship between skratching and developing electronic literacies is important to cool. Like hypertext, sampling, TV, or film, skratching creates its own literacy through cuts and breaks.

   For this assignment, design your own writing practice. Skratching does so by defamiliarizing a familiar object, the turntable. For this assignment, create a Web site that takes a familiar object from the major discipline you are studying (for example, a calculator for accounting, a test tube for chemistry) and defamiliarizes its usage so that the way the object becomes employed acts as a means to write.

   Your project doesn't have to actually show you writing with the object, but what it should do is establish the definitions and groundwork for how the object can be used as a communication device. The challenge of this assignment is to rethink the usage of tools you are probably overfamiliar with.
2. *The Web as Literacy Practice.* For this assignment, take the previous assignment one step further. Create a Web site that proposes the Web as a new literacy practice. While we'll discuss the Web in more detail in the next chapter, you can use this assignment as a means towards thinking ahead.

To do this project, you first will probably need to outline how the Web treats writing, how writers express themselves on the Web, and how readers come to view that information. In order to accomplish this, surf the Web, visit as many different types of sites as possible, and take notes on how they treat writing.

Then you will need to devise a plan describing how the Web is currently used and how it may be used in the future. As you consider its potential, you might want to focus on one or two specific industries or businesses that could use the Web for production and distribution of information in ways they aren't currently doing.

You may also want to demonstrate what you propose. Therefore, if you say the Web is a new literacy practice, you can provide examples in your writing by demonstrating applicable methods.

3. *Skratching*. In the last section of this chapter, we discussed how skratching can function rhetorically as a critical practice. Create a Web site that skratches a popular idea or cultural assumption (like "self-made man"). Use images, hyperlinks, refresh tags, and JavaScripts (like the rollover) to challenge those assumptions. On this book's Web site, you can find further instructions regarding how to use these types of HTML and JavaScript codes.

Chapter

13

The Web

Since its rise in popularity in 1992, the World Wide Web's usage has grown dramatically. The number of Web pages in existence has swelled from a few hundred to several million. With increased numbers of dial-up and high-speed connections to the Web as well as intensified familiarity with Web site creation, popular culture interests in the World Wide Web have proliferated as well. Often, personal Web sites are created as home pages or to support an individual's taste in popular culture. In the latter category, we can find Web sites devoted to musical bands, actors or actresses, or cartoon characters. At the end of this book, we'll discuss how these types of Web sites relate to cool.

As we saw in Chapter 2, one aspect of this Web expansion is increased attention to popular culture terminology like the word cool. Typically, such attention materializes in the cool lists trend. Cool, however, appears elsewhere. Cool has been used to describe technological innovation and future predictions. This chapter examines how cool and corporate development merge on the Web so that the end result predicts a futuristic, Web-based writing process. Businesses interested in the so-called technology boom that accompanied the Web's popularity see outlets for their economic plans in popular culture. One place where this activity occurs is Hewlett-Packard's concept of cooltown.

Cooltown

Computer manufacturer Hewlett-Packard envisions a future in which our lives are completely intertwined with technology. The company imagines a place where from morning to night we are connected to information through the clothes we wear, the cars we drive, the places we work, and the relationships we maintain, and it believes future technological investment will create a society where humans and machines are always connected. Hewlett-Packard named this mythical environment cooltown. On its Web site (http://www.cooltown.hp.com/mpulse/backissues/0601/0601-cooltown.asp), Hewlett-Packard explains the concept in detail:

> Welcome to cooltown, our vision of a technology future where people, places, and things are first class citizens of the connected world, wired and wireless—a place where e-services meet the physical world, where humans are mobile, devices and services are federated and context-aware, and everything has a Web presence. In cooltown, technology transforms human experience from consumer lifestyles to business processes by enabling mobility. Cooltown is infused with the energy of the online world, and Web-based appliances and e-services give you what you need when and where you need it for work, play, life.

Go to the cooltown Web site and see how Hewlett-Packard envisions a technology-rich future.

As the description makes clear, in cooltown, all movement will be controlled by computer technology created for the Internet. Hewlett-Packard's concept of cooltown capitalizes on computer developments that are making chips smaller and smaller every year. Small computers mean the machines can be put to work in places one wouldn't normally expect to find a computer, like a t-shirt or a button. The idea behind cooltown is that such expansions of technology in our daily lives will prove beneficial to our overall standard of living and life enjoyment. In cooltown, an automobile, for example, will utilize information distribution systems (like the Web or a similar network) to convey to its driver that a part is malfunctioning, while the car simultaneously phones ahead to a service station.

While cooltown may be an overly Utopian fantasy that assumes all peoples will have access to this fictionalized place, it does offer a useful conception of cool and of writing. Based on this above description and additional information available on its Web site, this Hewlett-Packard project appears to have two basic tenets that are relevant to our own writing.

- Mobility
- Interlinking of distinct activities (like ordering coffee and driving a car simultaneously)

Both ideas have long traditions in cool. Representations of cool in the 1950s, for example, often depicted mobile teenagers whose cars played important roles in their lives. The George Lucas film *American Graffiti* emphasizes this point. Representative of late 1950s and early 1960s American culture, its plot moves by way of the film's various car-laden scenes. Fights, romance, and comedy all revolve around the presence of an automobile. Indeed, car culture typically revolves around cool teenagers looking for adventure. Hewlett-Packard associates cool with the car-inspired metaphor of mobility. To communicate in cooltown, people will also be on the go.

Hewlett-Packard's vision of cool as an interlinking system stems (even if inadvertently) from media theorist Marshall McLuhan's work. To understand cooltown's rhetorical relevance to our own writing, we need to first look briefly at McLuhan's concept of cool.

In his 1964 book *Understanding Media*, McLuhan divided all media forms into two kinds: hot and cool. McLuhan based his definitions on the quality of a medium's definition and the amount of participation required to make sense of that definition. When reading a text or viewing an image, we always participate in the viewing and reading processes to some extent. McLuhan's interest was in the degree of participation required.

Hot media, McLuhan felt, are media with high definition that require little participation by viewers or readers in order to understand the content's meaning. Print and film are two examples of hot media. Reading a magazine or a book, one doesn't need to do much other than run one's eyes over the page. The words are already there. Participation is limited. When watching a film, we see the film image as single frames projected onto a screen. Little participation is required by viewers to combine the frames and make sense of the film's meaning.

Cool media, on the other hand, have low definition and thus require extensive participation. The telephone, for example, is cool because you need to speak into one end of the receiver in order to be heard on the other. In addition, in order to have a conversation, at least two people have to participate. McLuhan also called comics and cartoons cool because the character representations we see are not detailed enough to be realistic. We have to participate mentally in the reading process by filling in the gaps. Charlie Brown doesn't really look like a little boy. We mentally fill in the lines and reshape the caricature so that we can consider him a boy and not a drawing.

McLuhan claimed that cool media require so much participation that they force media forms to participate in each other's production and meaning. In other words, we can no longer think of individual subjects and ideas as having nothing to do with one another. Instead, we must see all ideas as interlinked. The process of interlinking biology and writing, for example, becomes a cool activity. Using a computer in a writing class is cool as well. Connecting your watch to the Internet also marks a cool activity. Think about how CNN *Headline News* juxtaposes sports updates, weather information, stock market news, and a daily report simultaneously on the television screen. CNN's news updates indicate a cool form of writing.

Based on McLuhan's definition, cool media rhetorically:

- Are low in definition
- Require high participation by viewers and readers
- Interlink with other media forms

McLuhan's work on media was formulated in the early 1960s, and much has changed since. Therefore, we don't need to test his theory by applying it exactly to every media form we come across. No doubt we can find discrepancies and gaps where the theory doesn't hold up entirely. Instead, we can generalize from his definition and use it to read media differently than we may be accustomed to doing. For example, how do advertisements create high levels of viewer participation (think back to the examples we provided in Chapter 6)? How does school work against McLuhan's ideas regarding cool or support them? How do business practices function or not function as cool systems?

With the advent of computer technology, McLuhan's ideas about media and cool appear very relevant to anyone interested in electronic writing. Technology allows for activities to connect in ways previously impossible. English classes often take place in computer classrooms. Americans can quickly discover information about Afghanistan's internally and externally fought wars. Through new technology, attitudes and ideas easily can be juxtaposed in new ways. Therefore, when we write in this always interlinking environment, the form and content of our writing should resemble the various connections being made around us. Thus, the CNN *Headline News* example demonstrates one company's attempt to write in a cool manner. We'll return to this example once more shortly.

Eventually, McLuhan's cool media demonstrates a commercial angle as well. By drawing upon cool's rich background, Hewlett-Packard portrays cool media as a commercial enterprise. Hewlett-Packard is a business. Its vision of cooltown involves increasing its ability to sell more of its products. If you visit the cooltown Web site and the development pages that outline the project's progress, you'll notice that in cooltown there is room for only one computer manufacturer. When Hewlett-Packard presents cool as a futuristic society where everything interlinks, they implicitly mean a place where *their* products interlink with our daily lives. The company poses a hypothetical example (detailed on its Web site) of how we will be able to avoid getting wet while catching a bus on a rainy day. The cooltown resident synchronizes her palm-sized computer with the bus' global positioning system, which links to the Web. Realizing she has plenty of time before the next bus arrives, she uses her computer to connect to a nearby coffee shop, orders a coffee, and pays for the coffee before she's even entered the shop. Since Hewlett-Packard imagines this version of cooltown, we can assume that Hewlett-Packard tools are capable of making the scenario a reality.

> What does it mean when a word like cool is used to describe the places in which we live, work, and entertain? Does Hewlett-Packard's concept of cooltown redefine how we use the word to identify ourselves? If we lived in cooltown, would we automatically be "cool" people? Would this completely change our notion of a cool person?

Hewlett-Packard's vision of cooltown uses cool to:

- Attract a young customer base by appropriating a word from popular culture (cool)
- Conceptualize an interlinking society that is cool because of the intricate ways it forms connections between distinct businesses and lifestyles

When a computer manufacturer adopts cool ideas to promote an ultra-modern society, the result still resembles what we saw in the beginning of this book, with the added dimension of interlinking. Visit Hewlett-Packard's Web site devoted to cooltown: http://www.cooltown.hp.com. Do you think people who will live in cooltown will walk around acting "cool" (i.e., wearing fashionable clothes or speaking slang)? Or will they be cool because of how they use technology to conduct their lives? What is the difference?

Commercialism and Technology

Hewlett-Packard's cooltown provides one example of how technology allows corporations to use cool as an electronic writing for economic means. As new technologies allow information to be spread quickly and to large audiences, many corporations can sell more of their products than they could previously. Electronic technology, like the World Wide Web, allows corporations that produce numerous products to sell a variety of goods connected to one theme at once, which is what Hewlett-Packard appears to be positioning itself to do. This marketing technique is called creating tie-ins. Tie-ins act like product placements; they use one product to attract attention to other products a company sells. One medium devoted to a given product subtly connects to another medium where another product is sold.

Movies are a good example of this process. When a major movie comes out, the film company producing and distributing the movie expects profits from more than the movie's ticket sales. Toys, books, CDs, clothes, posters, and various other items will be tied into the movie's release. Movie companies want to sell more than the movie; they want customers to purchase associated products as well. The interlinking of all these items with a film is an example of cool media taking place. The all-around inclusive nature of the media makes it cool, based on McLuhan's definition of cool. Sprite once ran a commercial that demonstrated how tie-ins work. A group of executives sit around a table discussing the release of their new film, *Death Slug*. The project coordinator asks each executive to present his proposed tie-in to the film. One shows a slug action figure, another slug slippers, and another slug-on-a-stick. When the coordinator asks how the movie is going, one executive replies, "Well, we don't have a script yet, but we can bang one out by Friday."

While the commercial parodies tie-ins, it also represents the economic aspect of interlinking we often forget about. The commercial suggests that the supposed "main attraction," the film itself, is less important than the commercial products created in accordance with the film. These products take innumerable forms. An interview or news story may in fact be a paid promotion for the film. Collector's items (cups, key chains, toys) are created solely to promote the film and provide additional revenue. Even a feature story in a major newspaper about a film may be a tie-in, an advertisement paid for by the movie company. Dissecting these intricate business relationships can be tricky. But if we are to become intelligent consumers and not just passive recipients of consumer culture, then we need to be aware of their existence. The question for cool consumers is at what point does one deconstruct the cool nature of tie-ins or give in and allow product placement to govern our purchasing habits?

Harry Potter and the Sorcerer's Stone was one of the biggest films of 2001. But how many products were tied in to the film's release? Where do you remember seeing feature stories about the film? In what magazines? On what TV shows?

Did you suddenly see an increasing number of children wearing Harry Potter glasses on TV? Did you see talk shows repeatedly referencing the movie in various ways? What is the relationship between these organizations and the producer of the film? Are they part of the same company? How do you feel when companies saturate a number of different media forms with one product? Is there a rhetoric towards creating tie-ins?

Because the Web has attracted considerable attention from the business world, it also has become an important vehicle for propagating tie-ins. Both CNN's news network and Web site offer another good example of how tie-ins work. Research into CNN's management structure reveals that AOL Time Warner owns CNN. On its network news programs, CNN often features entertainment stories with subheadings for *People* magazine. *People* is one of AOL Time Warner's holdings. *People's* Web site features a Netscape navigation bar at the top of its page. AOL Time Warner also owns Netscape. On CNN's site, you can find ads for *Time* magazine and *Sports Illustrated* (also AOL Time Warner companies). Looking over these relationships, if you weren't aware all of these companies are, in fact, one company, you might think that corporate cooperation exists. You might also believe that *People's* appearance on CNN results from the magazine's newsworthy stories. In fact, *People's* repetitive mentioning on CNN stems from the two companies' financial relationship. These corporations utilize digital media to interlink their products. But why?

- To establish a common customer base
- To advertise two or more products simultaneously

The aftereffect of cool media, therefore, creates excessive interlinking of different organizations and their production in ways possibly misleading to the consumers purchasing their products. The types of writing that occur in *People* magazine or on CNN's Web site use a cool method in a transparent way. The intent is to expose an audience to a number of publications at once without revealing their common relationship.

Another result from this process is greater homogeneity in production. Target audiences become reduced to specific groups whose tastes are styled to the producer's interests. Consequently, companies strive to keep their output similar and, therefore, cost-effective. With technological innovations, cool production leads to a marketplace where everything slowly becomes the same.

As we noted early in this book, Internet tie-ins, especially those based on cool, flourish on the Web. For instance, Yahoo.com's coverage of the 2002 Grammy awards lists all of the ceremony's winners. When viewers click the link to a specific winner, they're taken to Yahoo's companion site, Launch, where they can listen to short clips from the winner's album or even purchase the album. Yahoo also runs the site where most of the music can be bought. Utilizing the cool, interconnected nature of the Web, Yahoo constructs a direct path to its retail services. As consumers of music (and other products promoted on the Web and sold through its various portals), do we pay attention to these multifaceted connections? When we click hyperlinks, do we take note and examine who links to whom? Do we recognize if a site that appears different is, in fact, the same site as the one we just visited?

> See how many tie-ins you can identify. First, identify how a specific movie, fast-food chain, news service, or retailer connects its products to other products its parent company sells. Then apply the same test to the Web. Locate several news-based sites, and see which incorporate tie-ins and which don't.
>
> Does there seem to be any logic to the differences? Does the size of the company supporting the site matter?

Sometimes, even those who deride cool as a consumer industry become intertwined in its economic structure. You may recall that in Chapter 4 we read about Douglas Rushkoff's association with PBS, who produced his documentary, *The Merchants of Cool*. In his film, Rushkoff critiques the tie-in process extensively for how it masks as "freedom of choice." As we've been doing in this section, Rushkoff makes clear that participants of consumer culture often don't "choose" products; instead corporations promote their products as if they come from a variety of avenues, when in fact they come from one company. *The Merchants of Cool*, however, is also somewhat guilty of this process. PBS' Web site accompanies the documentary and also functions as a tie-in. We previously noted the "shop" link the site maintains. In addition, each time regional stations broadcast the show, they draw attention to the PBS Web site. In turn, the Web site ties-in to other PBS shows, including other shows that are part of the *Frontline* series, like *The Merchants of Cool*.

Other Web sites play off the traditional attitudes associated with cool youth in order to take advantage of tie-ins. Absolut.com uses drinking as a lure. Visitors to its site can use the site's Flash technology to play games, make their own films, and watch company videos. The highly interactive nature of the site updates McLuhan's vision of cool as media promoting participation. But it also encourages the tie-in philosophy strongly related to cool and technology. By playing games and making movies, visitors, Absolut hopes, will be more inclined to purchase the company's vodka.

All of these examples detail cool writing as an economic activity. In our writing classes, we won't use cool for commercial purposes. However, we can consider how the cool tie-in can be generalized to other forms of writing relevant to our work as students of electronic writing. And because a great deal of Web writing involves using hyperlinks to connect Web pages, we can use tie-ins in our writing in order to forge complex connections that will persuade our readers to agree with points we want to make.

- What examples of tie-ins can you think of? Search the Internet or spend time watching TV news channels like CNN, E!, or MSNBC. How do they create tie-ins that are specific enough to encourage consumers to buy the product, but not too blunt to turn viewers off?
- Do tie-ins take advantage of viewers/consumers? Or are they the result of the natural tendencies of a system with more resources than ever? In other words, as technology makes interlinking easier and easier, can we avoid this type of advertising?
- How do hyperlinks give company Web sites increased opportunity to create tie-ins?
- How do we relate the tie-in phenomenon to our own writing? We're not trying to sell products, but can we use the concept of tie-ins differently; that is, can tie-ins allow us additional options in connecting complex ideas, background information, related material, etc. when we write?
- Think of a typical writing assignment you've done in the past. How did you provide background information to your topic? How did you present your supports or your research? Could you have done a hypertextual version of the same writing but with tie-ins motivating the form of your essay instead of paragraph by paragraph structure?

Further Reading

McLuhan, Marshall. *The Medium Is the Massage*. San Francisco: Hardwired, 1996 (1967).

———. *Understanding Media*. New York: Signet, 1964.

Tomorrow Never Looked So Cool." *Wired News* 23 June 2001. http://www.wired.com/news/gizmos/0,1452,44676,00.html?tw=wn20010623

Web Site

On this book's Web site, you can find further examples of tie-ins and links to companies that have complex commercial relationships with other companies, but who keep that information low key.

Class Discussion

1. Should we be concerned when large corporations like Hewlett-Packard appropriate the language of popular culture in uncritical ways? Or should we welcome such moves as a recognition of popular culture's influence on mainstream society?
2. What does the inclusion of McLuhan's definition of cool do to the previous meanings we've explored in this book? How does it add to or change those definitions?
3. As a class, discuss how cool can be a media form and not just a personality trait or status symbol.

Exercises

1. *The Cool System.* Based on our discussion of cooltown and McLuhan's notion of cool as the interlinking of distinct ideas, methods, practices, or writings, design a cool system of communication for a specific business, school, industry, or family situation on a Web site.

   This assignment asks you to think how you can change a current system of communication that is "hot" (that is, it doesn't allow for different ideas or methods to be connected) and propose a way to make it "cool."

   Create a Web site that both describes this design and shows it. Preferably, you will use the Web site to show the cool system you create in action.

2. *The Tie-In.* Our final comments in this chapter proposed tie-ins as a model for writing. This assignment asks you to put our initial conjecture to practice by creating an argumentative tie-in essay.

   Based on your instructor's direction regarding topic selection, write an argumentative essay for the Web. First outline your project according to traditional argumentation:

   Introduction (background/problem's history/previous approaches to problem)

   Claim (or thesis)

   Supporting evidence (research, examples)

   Refutation of opposing viewpoints (optional)

   Conclusion (not a summation, but a place for further inquiry)

   Instead of laying out these ideas in a paragraph by paragraph structure, use hyperlinks as tie-ins to fulfill each part of the essay's framework. You might have, for example, an introduction page that begins the essay, but various links off that page will function as tie-ins to your project's background or history. The tie-ins will take words, ideas, or implicit points raised in your introduction and connect the rest of the argumentative structure the way tie-ins typically do on the Web.

   For further evidence of tie-ins, return to the questions this chapter asks and find more examples on the Internet and in newspapers, news broadcasts, or films.

Chapter

14

Cyberculture

The question of how tie-ins affect digital writing extends into the vast area commonly referred to as cyberculture. In cyberculture, the medium of the World Wide Web interlinks a vast amount of material typically unrelated yet represented through Web pages, Weblogs, chat rooms, animation, video, games, and file sharing. When brought together, the various items we find in these places construct a strange, online environment where virtuality, technology, science fiction, and the everyday combine. What is cyberculture? It's a term that, like cool, maintains different meanings for different people. Mass media representations of cyberculture include the film *Blade Runner*, hypertext, William Gibson's novel *Neuromancer*, e-mail, chat rooms, *Robocop*, video games, *Wired* magazine, home pages, instant messaging, computer hackers, cell phones, *The Matrix*, and industrial music, among other items.

If the various items that comprise cyberculture have anything in common, it is their propensity to merge technology with other forms of expression or with cultural items that can exist independently of new technology. Police officers, for instance, don't have to be robots, but *Robocop* juxtaposes the two as it attempts to explain what has become of law enforcement in the not too distant future. While distinct, all of these items together construct an image of cyberculture as:

- Futuristic
- Building upon old forms
- Interconnected
- Often strange and unsettling when first introduced

Science fiction novelist William Gibson describes cyberspace, the locale of cyberculture, as a "consensual hallucination experienced daily by billions of legitimate operators, in every nation, by children being taught mathematical concepts...a graphic representation of data abstracted from the banks of every computer in the human system" (51). Gibson wrote this description in *Neuro-mancer*, his 1984 prophetic vision of the Web, eight years before the Web was created. Even then, Gibson saw technology as a force that would eventually control our daily experiences. At the same time, Gibson attributed to cyberspace the quality of being a "hallucination." Cyberspace creates an imaginary place where its participants believe they are experiencing reality, when, in fact, they may or may not be doing so.

In *Neuromancer*, the space cowboy Case uses a portable, computer-styled system to "jack in" to cyberspace, a computer environment constructed from accumulated data and information banks. Today, the Web represents Gibson's image of cyberspace. The Web exists as nothing more than assorted bits and pieces of information stored on computers worldwide. We access that data by logging on to the Internet (in place of jacking in) and viewing this information in the form of Web pages. When you surf the Internet, you are, in fact, moving through significant quantities of information arranged in various places and in various patterns.

What makes cyberculture cool? Our first reactions to a well-designed Web site or flashy use of technology on the Web might, in fact, be "cool!" In addition to this initial perception of the Web and cyberculture, however, we can apply McLuhan's understanding of cool media. In his book *Escape Velocity*, Mark Dery uses McLuhan's theory to investigate the various items that incorporate cyberculture. Dery collects information on items he believes comprise cyberculture: raves, tattoo artists, performance artists like Stelarc and Orlan, bot wars, the cyberpunk movement, cyber sex, movies, industrial rock, and real life cyborgs. Dery calculates that together these items function as conjoined places of expression that interlink with one another in often unintentional ways. Cyberculture, therefore, is fundamentally cool, like some of the other technology inventions we've discussed, for creating a highly participatory atmosphere. For Dery, this participation is rooted in popular culture, art, and science. When viewed in conjunction with another, these three areas turn cyberspace into a collage.

Collage is an artistic practice of cutting and pasting unlike items (visual and textual) into a single "frame" in order to produce an alternative representation. Looking at a collage, viewers must form associations and create meaning more so than if they were looking at a very representational image, such as a still life or a portrait. While we always construct meanings from imagery, a portrait is very explicit about what it represents (a person). A collage leaves the meaning as more ambiguous; the responsibility to make sense of the representation lies with the viewer's willingness to participate in its creation. In this way, we can consider collages as unfinished works that become complete only when we, the readers or viewers, determine their meanings. When we refer to cyberspace as a collage, we propose that to make sense of cyberspace media, like the Web, we must become active participants in its creation and proliferation.

Collage has become a widely used method of expression in our media-based culture. Find collagist examples in magazines you read, advertisements you watch, films you've seen, and in even in music you hear.

What do these applications of collage have in common? Can you construct a list of collage's attributes by carefully examining these items?

Following Dery's logic, cyberspace's first widely used medium, the World Wide Web, is a cool place for communication. The ways we use this medium must be cool as well if we want anybody to understand what we desire to communicate. Consequently, we need to acclimatize how we write for print culture to the demands of cool media. In the 1960s, Marshall McLuhan worried that in the digital age, writers would apply the tools of print culture to cool media without any adjustment. He argued that if the tools of print culture were systematically applied to digital culture, the results would not be effective. To demonstrate how writing must become collagist and cool, McLuhan wrote books that adapted the collage form. His *Understanding Media* and *The Medium Is the Massage* are collages of cut and paste quotations, sections, and in the latter book, images. McLuhan challenged writing, and in particular academic writing, to embrace forms of expression in line with digital production. McLuhan felt that schools should teach writing as collage because this medium better reflects how digital culture operates.

Take an assignment you had to do in another class, in which you wrote in a linear, paragraph-by-paragraph way. Following McLuhan's idea about writing and collage, turn this assignment into a collage. Use text and image to construct your collage.

What's different? What's the same? Are there alternative ways to making your point that are impossible to express in words? Are there things you could do in words that you can't do in a collage?

Cyberspace as Hypertext

Tim Berners-Lee, the inventor of the World Wide Web, had an idea similar to McLuhan's. Working at CERN (the European Particle Physics Laboratory located in Geneva, Switzerland) in the 1980s (before the Web's creation), Berners-Lee noticed that the organization's scientists tended to work in isolation from one another. As a result, projects were being duplicated. A scientist with a project that could benefit from someone else's work and insight had no idea that the other work existed, and much effort and energy was going to waste. To deal with this problem, Berners-Lee wrote Enquire, a program that could record connections among projects and people at CERN. This was his first effort at creating Web-like software. With Enquire, CERN's scientists could see how their work was interrelated. Eventually Enquire, along with subsequent programs Berners-Lee created, led to the World Wide Web, a space located on the Internet that utilizes hypertext's ability to link distinct subject matter together. In *Weaving the Web*, his account of how he developed the World Wide Web, Berners-Lee recalls his initial motivation for writing the initial Enquire program. "Suppose all the information stored on computers everywhere were linked, I thought. Suppose I could program my computer to create a space in which anything could be linked to anything."

The Web fulfills Berners-Lee's project mostly by creating a space where hyperlinks can forge associations and connections between different places of information. Berners-Lee's project resembles McLuhan's work to a great extent, especially in the desire to interlink unrelated information in order to demonstrate how information connects in subtle and provocative ways. To understand Berners-Lee's vision of an interlinking writing space as cool and to be able to apply that vision to our own writing, we need to visit a few Web sites and writing spaces. Like our other examples of cool media, the ensuing discussion is not meant to be inclusive, but merely a sampling of what exists. We encourage you to discover other sites that might exemplify cool better than those displayed here. Moreover, our choices are not endorsements of these sites; their selection is based merely on their relative "coolness" regarding this discussion of hypertext and cyberculture.

First we'll look at a commercial Web site where distinct pieces of writing are united under one umbrella name. Then we'll examine a membership-based Web site where multiple writings exist in connection with one another. You should visit these sites on your own in order to get a more concrete image of how they function.

For our first discussion, we'll look at CBS SportsLine.

- Go to the Web site at http://www.sportsline.com/.
- Look over the various headlines and identify one you want to read about.
- Click through the link and read over what follows. Take notes on what you've read, how you found this information, who wrote this information, and how the information was displayed.
- Either go back to the main page or follow another link (one that will keep you at SportsLine) on the page you currently are reading.
- Read over this page and repeat the same process until you've looked at several different pages.

What is your initial reaction to how SportsLine presents content to its readers? What do your notes tell you about the site's methodology for building a resource center of sports-related data?

Like the CBS news programs, SportsLine adopts a newspaper-styled format for delivering its content to readers. SportsLine looks a lot like a newspaper. Newspapers divide the main pages of each section into headlines. Readers track the headlines by following instructions at the bottom of an incomplete article (for example, "continued on page 3D") and by flipping through the section to the page where the story continues. On SportsLine, readers do the same by clicking through links or by using the pull-down menu at the top of the page for navigation.

SportsLine resembles other commercial Web sites like CNN.com because it claims to be a unified information service, but different people write its articles. On the Web site's home page, links connect the reader to individual stories regarding football, basketball, hockey, and other sports. Below the links a short description sometimes identifies the author of the hyperlinked news story. Often, however, the author's name is absent. As we click through the various headlined stories, we read distinct authorial perspectives. While SportsLine positions itself as a single-entity authorial presence by way of its bold title, its content is, in fact, created by a number of individual writers who likely work in isolation of one another (sometimes in different states or countries). Like Berners-Lee's vision of the Web as an interlinking space, SportsLine forges connections between these varied writers by making sure each links either to one another or to the main page. The site's coolness derives from how it creates these connections.

How do we read a site like this? What do you recall the most after reading through several pages on a site like Sportsline? Do you remember the author's name or the story's content? How do the links distinguish who is writing what? As you click from page to page within the site, and as you consequently read various articles, do you have the impression you are reading one writer's work or several? What would happen if you read the front page as one single document? Would the site still make sense? Would you be able to understand any of the text? Mentally switch the order of how the headlines and images appear on the main page. Does order matter?

All of these questions can get us to think of Web sites as cool, interactive sites of information. How sites like SportsLine arrange information and present it affects audiences in very specific ways. For instance, fragmenting articles into short headlines on the front page is meant to get our attention so that we will enter the site and read further. Placing a number of links to articles regarding, for instance, the NCAA men's basketball Final Four (if you are looking at Sportsline.com in March) on the same page attempts to draw connections between the different writers' positions. All of these writers, however, may be in disagreement, may not know of the other's work, or may be, in fact, collaborating. However they write these articles, SportsLine creates an image that implies that their work is connected in some way.

This kind of writing challenges our assumptions about what it means to identify writing by its author. If we fail to recognize that each piece of writing stands independent of the next, then the rhetorical effect causes us to emphasize the writing over its author. What might be the advantages or disadvantages of this kind of writing? And for whom would this be advantageous or disadvantageous?

As a class, pick a subject like sports, movies, television, music, etc. Each member writes a short description or headline about a relevant figure or event in the chosen area. No one signs their name to what's been written. After everyone finishes writing, assemble the writings together as one text.

How well (or not) do the selections work together? Do they cohere? Do they seem out of place with one another?

Who should claim responsibility for authoring this text? Each individual writer? The person who assembled the fragmented pieces of writing? The person (or persons) who chose the subject to write about?

In contrast to SportsLine.com, we'll now look at another site that is cool for how it interlinks writings in a different manner. In Chapter 2, we briefly mentioned how the Web site Everything2.com employs cool to describe the interlinking writing on their site. Everything2.com is another good place to test Berners-Lee's concept.

- Go to http://www.everything2.com.
- Follow a node on either the left side of the screen or in the middle.
- After reading through the node, pick a highlighted word (one of the links) and click through. Take notes about what you read.
- Read through the new node that appears. Then pick another word and click through. Continue taking notes about what you read.
- Repeat the process until you have a considerable amount of notes.
- Look through your notes. Circle common terms, words, and ideas. In other words, circle the patterns connecting the nodes you've read.

Did you move through the same word each time, or did you choose different words? What common pattern links all of the nodes you read through? How do all the nodes you read connect? What does it mean to find a pattern in writings authored by distinct individuals at different time periods?

As one example, we began with a node entitled "If I get taxed in my job, why can't I vote? (idea)," which discussed issues of equal rights and the Constitution. Clicking on the word "race" in the node, we then read a poem about ostracism called "Race," and then clicked through the word "people." This link took us to several usages of the word people, including a brief definition, a translation of the poem "People" by Yevgeny Yevtushenko, and lyrics from a song called "People." After reading the nodes and looking over our notes on them, we saw that each of these three nodes, all written by different people, connect various understandings of rights, race, individuality, and discrimination. They do so by drawing upon public documents like the Constitution, poetry, song lyrics, and through other nodes, by linking to clichés, personal anecdotes, and geographical descriptions. What we found is that, when read in juxtaposition with one another by clicking through hyperlinks, a variety of different texts can yield a common idea.

Everything2.com, then, is cool because it encourages active participation among the site's contributors. Writers don't work independently to create knowledge; instead, they participate in knowledge production by building on each other's work. This may sound strange to you if most of your writing experience has been in school classrooms via timed assignments or assignments that asked you to "do your own work." In a typical classroom, your desks are separate, you use your own paper, and talking tends to be disallowed. In some classrooms, collaboration is discouraged because instructors believe collaborative work makes it too difficult for the instructor to determine who did what in the final product. In this scenario, writing is judged on its individual merit, not on its ability to connect to outside writings. Everything2.com's *cooling* of hypertext asks us to write otherwise. It asks us to work together, to interlink our thoughts in order to create meaning, and to see our ideas as connected to other ideas being disseminated.

All Web sites, however, connect ideas and writings through hyperlinks. How does Everything2.com connect distinct writings differently than SportsLine? How do Everything2.com's noders work in conjunction with one another in ways SportsLine's reporters don't? Do the two sites differ at all?

- Without labeling one site as better than the other, make a list describing how each differs from the other.
- As a class, discuss these differences and their effects on you, each site's audience.

Hypertext and Participation

Everything2.com constitutes an example of hypertext as cool for its ability to interlink. We can also consider hypertext as cool for the ways it creates high levels of interaction (remember McLuhan's complete definition of cool media?). Earlier in this chapter, we noted an association between cyberculture and collage. Referring to cyberculture as a collage of various media forms indicates a high level of participation by those who either engage with cyberculture or attempt to make sense of its numerous manifestations. Hypertext, too, can be collagist. Some applications of hypertext create high reader involvement, at a level that exceeds common reading experience. After all, whether we read a printed book or a hypertext, we are also involved in the reading process to some extent. When we read a book, for instance:

- We have to choose the book.
- We have to open the book.
- We have to turn the pages.
- We have to figure out what the sentences say and what they mean.

All of this activity causes us to be involved with the text at some level. Similarly, when we log onto the Web and visit a Web site:

- We have to turn on the computer and open the browser we use to surf the Web.
- We have to locate the Web site by typing in the URL or doing a search for it.
- We have to click through links to navigate from one part of the site to another.

For the most part, this is a common Web reading experience. The SportsLine.com and Everything2.com examples present two different approaches some sites take in order to expand these experiences. Some Web sites, however, go beyond the types of hypertextual applications we've seen with SportsLine or Everything2.com. With the two sites we've examined, meaning can be deciphered fairly easily by following hyperlinks. Other types of Web sites use hypertext provocatively so that readers will have to spend time navigating through dense interlinking, juxtapositions, and imagery before any meaning can be evaluated. Often, experimental or artistic Web sites use hypertext in this way. Among these sites, Rhizome.org, Jodi.org, and Trashconnection.com exemplify hypertextual writing that, at first, may appear dense and obscure. We can once again test these Web sites' coolness by noting how much effort we need to apply to understand what the sites say.

- Go to http://www.jodi.org.
- Make note of what you see.
- Get off the site by going to another Web site entirely (it doesn't matter which).
- Go to http://www.jodi.org again (if you see the same thing you saw the first time, close your browser and log into the site once more).
- What's changed? Is this the same site? Jodi.org alters the home page each time a visitor enters the site. From the start, visitor perception is challenged as we have to try to figure out where we are, why the site looks different, and what will happen next.
- Explore the site and make notes about what you see. How does Jodi.org differ from more conventional Web sites like CNN.com and ESPN.com? All of these sites use hypertext. Why do they look so different? Which is harder to understand? Why?
- Would you call what you've read "strange" or "weird"? Do you think it's just noise? The easiest answer to these questions is "yes." What initially seems different we might dismiss as unimportant or ridiculous. But let's assume there is a purpose to what the writers at Jodi.org are doing. Look at the details of what you read. Do you see some purpose? Do you see a pattern? Pay attention to the site's details.

- What kind of audience do you imagine the creators of this site are attempting to reach? Do you consider yourself as part of that audience? Why or why not? Why would a different audience be more inclined to find meaning here than you? Which audience?
- Come up with three to four responses that question what the site is doing and what the writings you looked at might be about. You can phrase your responses as a question, if you prefer.

Whether you like Jodi.org or not, its alternative usage of hypertext demonstrates how cool's participatory characteristic can provoke emotional responses from readers, even if that response involves a sense of bewilderment. Getting your reader to feel something means appealing to the reader's *pathos*, a Greek rhetorical term for emotional plea. If these experimental sites make you uncomfortable, frustrated, or perplexed, then they've done a good job with pathos in a very contemporary manner.

These sites also conceive of discourse as allusive. The sites lack exact points or claims; their purpose is undefined. To make sense of the site's focus, we must construct our own meanings by choosing among the chaotic texts and imagery the sites display. In this case, cool writing can be ambiguous. Readers actively participate in deciphering the text's meaning by coming to terms with its ambiguity and allusive nature.

> Think of three to four texts you've encountered in the past and which you felt were allusive in meaning (other than Web sites). They can be movies, photos, novels, poems, newspaper articles, advertisements, or something else.
>
> Why were these texts allusive? How did you eventually arrive at a meaning while reading these texts? Would you classify your participation in deciphering these texts as cool? Why or why not?

Does it strike you as odd that a writing textbook draws attention to writing that lacks specificity? Isn't all writing supposed to be specific in its content, as well as clear and concise in its delivery? Yes and no. Many writing situations demand that our ideas be delivered as clear and coherent. Specific classes you take or specific tasks you perform outside of school may ask you to be clear and coherent. The sites we've looked at in this chapter demonstrate a need for writing that isn't entirely clear. When we encounter writing that lacks clarity, we need to ask who this writing is intended for, why it lacks coherence, and what its overall rhetorical effect is. We also need to ask what situations might require us to write in ambiguous ways in order to be persuasive.

These Web sites provide one of many examples of writing that isn't clear (William S. Burroughs and the Situationists, who we discussed earlier, are two other examples). If we brush off this type of writing as irrelevant and nonsense, we run the risk of dismissing too quickly new approaches to media writing.

It might be more beneficial to situate these sites within the history of new approaches to writing. When the French writer Montaigne first introduced the essay form in the sixteenth century, intellectual response considered his work as confusing, unorganized, and lacking proper form. The novel's early beginnings in the seventeenth century provoked similar responses. Initially, critics deemed the novel as an inferior form of writing, as only appropriate for female audiences because of its lack of intellectual content, and as not worth scholarly attention. At that time, to consider the novel as a text for analysis or cultural evaluation would have seemed ludicrous. Educators deemed novels as having little value to share. Today, we study the novel in English classes without thinking about its past reception, and we have raised specific novels to the level of artistic greatness. More specifically, American literature didn't become a subject for serious study until late in the nineteenth century, even though a significant body of writings existed previously, and it didn't fully become a part of most school curriculums until the twentieth century. Compared to classical English literature, American literature was classified as too popular or lacking in artistic merit.

Typically, school systems no longer question literature's importance to English studies or a liberal arts education, nor do they question having students write essays. Most colleges and universities require students to take literature classes regardless of their chosen majors. Literature's high level of acceptability today exists despite its tumultuous beginnings. We're not saying that Web sites like Jodi.org will one day reach the same cultural and intellectual status as the essay or the novel. Instead, we draw attention to how initial perception of alternative forms may cause people to reject such efforts as lacking substance. With time, the initial shock wears off, audiences come to understand the forms better, and eventually, audiences often treat the forms as models for emulation.

By identifying experimental Web sites as cool, we also don't want to dismiss the importance of writing clearly to a specific audience within a specific context (a resume, a memo, a letter of thanks, a critical analysis of a text, etc.). Instead, we want to see how writers can also deliver positions without being clear about their purpose. Allusiveness, then, operates as a cool, rhetorical strategy. By being allusive, these kinds of writers place an alternative responsibility upon their readers to become more engaged in the reading process. In this case, cool's rhetorical value lies in how it prompts a unique form of participation.

Further Reading

Mark Amerika's Alt-X network. http://www.alt-x.org

Calvino, Italo. *If on a Winter Night, a Traveler*. New York: Harvest, 1981.

Derry, Mark. *Escape Velocity: Cyberculture at the End of the Century*. New York: Grove Press, 1996.

Gibson, William. *Neuromancer*. New York: Ace Books, 1984.

McLuhan, Marshall. *The Medium Is the Massage*. San Francisco: Hardwired, 1996 (1967).

———. *Understanding Media*. New York: Signet, 1964.

Noon, Jeff. *Pixel Juice*. New York: Doubleday, 1998.

Web Site

Not discussed in this chapter but relevant to the connection between cool and the Web are Weblogs. Weblogs are highly interactive places on the Web where writers keep track of their ideas, note daily events important to them, and link to other Weblogs on the Internet. Writing is posted as daily entries, and readers often have the option to offer comments to what they've read. Weblogs also combine the familiar with the unfamiliar. Go to this book's Web site for further information regarding Weblogs (including how to set one up) and for links to various Weblogs you can visit.

Class Discussion

1. Spend more time surfing through the sites we mention in this chapter. As a class, discuss why these sites disturb or don't disturb you. What is the rhetorical value of being disturbed?

2. What kinds of Web sites do you prefer to read? Do you prefer sites that are clear or sites that are allusive? Why?

Exercises

1. *The Collage Assignment*. Much of what we've discussed in this chapter argues that collage is a method cyberculture uses to construct meaning. Collages are typically allusive because they don't work for a specific statement or point; they leave meanings to be defined by readers.

   For this assignment, you will construct a hypertextual collage of text, images, and HTML coding that reflects an idea you have, position you hold regarding a specific issue, or interest. Your choice for subject matter on which to base your collage is open-ended. But your collage must use HTML.

2. *The Temporal Collage Assignment*. This assignment is more specific than the first. For this assignment, you will construct a hypertextual collage based on a temporal moment. This assignment's purpose is not to prove a causality between distinct moments in a given year, but to show how patterns can reveal new insights into previous cultural moments—much in the way Everything2.com's distinct writings operate by way of patterns.

3. First you need to pick a year. Any year will do: 1979, 1945, 1983, etc.

   Take note of the events that occurred in that year. Choose your events from a variety of subject areas and disciplines. These might include, but are not limited to comics, history, politics, films, TV shows, music, sports, science, fashion, etc. When you have a long list of events, pick four or five events you want to work with.

Research those events in great detail. Take good notes on what you discover about each event. It's important to note the various details that comprise the event.

Search for a pattern in your notes. What word, idea, concept, or belief reappears in each event you've researched?

When you've discovered the pattern, use that idea or phrase to develop a claim for an argument. Your supports for the argument are in the research you've done to generate this pattern.

Construct a hypertextual collage out of your research and claim that demonstrates the argument.

Chapter

15

Celebrity

This book began with a definition of cool we recognized as familiar: the cool person. One of cool's most typical usages is the identification of an individual as special for being unique, rebellious, allusive, tough, or some other feature. Because we began with the question of cool and personality, it seems appropriate to return once again to this subject.

For our final examination of cool and technology, we return to where we began in this book—with the image of the cool person. Since identifying a cool or not cool person was our initial, limited understanding of the word when we first picked up this book, thinking about cool individuals and the Web seems an appropriate place to conclude. Let's finish where we began, but let's do so by applying what we've learned. How do the various definitions of what makes someone cool translate when applied to the Web? How does the Web contribute to our recognition of cool people? How does it serve as a medium of expression for cool people? What happens to cool people in cyberspace?

The first step toward addressing these questions might be to look inward at ourselves and our relationship to the Web. Most of our first Web writing experiences began with creating a home page. Home pages are individual sites on the Web where we can talk about our interests, tastes, hobbies, achievements, and any other personal items. Even though a significant amount of space on the Web is devoted to commercial endeavors, the home page still exists as a small place for individual expression.

Companies like Geocities, Tripod, and Angelfire offer free Web hosting for their users to post home pages, thus making it easier than ever for anyone with a computer and Internet access to claim a Web presence. In turn, the Web has become populated with millions of personal home pages. By reading these pages, we can learn about someone we've never met and most likely never will meet. Yet, even though we don't know the person on an intimate level, by reading the individual's home page, we can also acquire some form of insight into a stranger's life so that we eventually feel we know this person. Relationships, then, become formed without any personal interaction. We've never met; and you know who I am; and consequently, I know who you are.

In some ways, when we put up a home page, we fulfill pop artist Andy Warhol's declaration that "in the future, everyone will be famous for fifteen minutes." When Warhol made this statement, he referred to technology's propensity to replicate and distribute imagery and text with ease to a large-scale audience, thus creating instant public recognition. With the home page, a sense of instant celebrity develops. Anyone can see me, learn about me, and if desired, emulate me. Suddenly, as in the neighborhood bar on the TV show *Cheers*, everybody knows my name. And how I present my name depends on what I want my home page to accomplish. As cyberculture critic Jay David Bolter notes in his essay "Identity," "The World Wide Web, too, permits us to construct our identities in and through the sites that we create as well as those that we visit." Web sites, like the home page, allow us specialized locales for constructing identity. By putting ourselves online, we also position such identities as pseudo celebrities.

How many personal home pages can you locate in ten minutes of Web searching? In thirty minutes?

How many students in your class have a home page (or had one before the semester began)? How many faculty in the department you belong to have home pages? How many faculty in your college or university have home pages?

Depending on how many you locate, what do you make of this number? Is it too large or too small?

As noted at the end of the last chapter in the Web site section, Weblogs are a new version of the home page. Visit this book's Web site for examples of Weblogs and how they differ from traditional home pages.

Issues of celebrity have often accompanied technological innovations in writing. The invention of the printing press, for example, created authorial celebrity. Prior to the printing press, books and other pieces of writing were not always identified by the name of the person who wrote them. Instead, handwritten manuscripts assembled a number of writings together in one book and listed each piece of writing by its title, not the author's name. And if the work was identified by an author's name, the entire collection often was referred to by the first name appearing in the book. Even if a collection represented ten or more different writers, the whole book might only be known by one author's name.

With the printing press came authorial recognition. The printing press also created various parts of the book we no longer pay much attention to, but which remain important to publishing, like title pages. The title page marks the place where the author identifies him or herself. Since printed books were in greater circulation and read by more people than handwritten manuscripts, through the title page, authors' names entered cultural vocabularies at larger rates. In turn, celebrity was created. Instead of referring to a piece of writing only by the title's name, readers could refer to authors' names as well. It wasn't long before certain authors became well-known figures to the increasing number of people who were able to read.

We can also see similar activity on the Web today. A home page constructed on a personal computer in the privacy of one's home is uploaded to a Web server where it becomes a Web site. Before long, it may be picked up by a search engine, linked to by another site, join a Web ring, and eventually be read by thousands of people.

Search engines allow for amplified exposure of one's name in cyberspace. Type your name into a search engine like Google or Dogpile. Does it come up? How many times?

How many of the hits refer to you and how many to other people with your name? When you find your name indexed on the Web, do you then feel famous? Why or why not?

Has someone ever contacted you after coming across your name, Web site, or something you wrote that was posted on the Web? Did this make you feel a bit famous?

Entertainment Celebrities

The Web also allows celebrity admiration to occur at an enhanced rate. With the increasing number of Web pages on the Internet comes a significant number of sites devoted to celebrities. As "fan" sites, these Web pages usually express awe for the celebrity, list the celebrity's films, books, or albums, or even detail the celebrity's personal life. The celebrity Web site phenomenon is not limited to individuals. TV shows, musical groups, and even commercial products all have Web sites devoted to them. Yahoo.com, for instance, indexes 13,166 sites devoted to actresses and actors. Among its vast database of information, the extensive index includes sites offering Jennifer Aniston's biography, interviews with Charlie Sheen, or John Travolta's filmography. The sites provide an information service, updating fans on a celebrity's latest work or developments in his or her personal life. In addition to this informational service, these Web sites treat celebrities as cool figures because of their name recognition and cultural status. By doing so, they *fetishize* celebrities.

Fetish is a word borrowed from psychology. It refers to a displacement of affection. When we cherish an object (and this includes treating a person like an object) in ways that replace the typical emotional expression devoted for people we know, we turn that object into a fetish. When we fetishize someone or something, we express emotion in a manner typically reserved for personal interaction. Tabloids, for instance, devote considerable effort towards diverting our emotions to celebrities. Tabloid gossip about celebrity alcoholism, adultery, and criminal mischief virtually involves us in strangers' lives. We don't know these people, and yet, at the same time, we do. Their image, their history, their personal lives may be quite familiar to us. In this sense, we become emotionally attached to people who we know only through their image. We fetishize celebrity through our fascination with tabloid news.

The tabloid format grew out of the newspaper, which itself was once a new innovation in information distribution. Contemporary tabloids like *National Enquirer*, *Weekly World News*, and *The Star* proliferate fetishized interest in celebrities by utilizing the newspaper's ability to reach a large audience immediately. Television acts as a cousin to the tabloid's celebrity fascination. Like the newspaper, television assisted in raising interest in celebrity. Because so many homes own a television set, one's appearance on a given show can lead to immediate celebrity status.

Think about how people become celebrities without any achievements or accomplishments. Merely appearing on television introduces their names and images to millions of Americans simultaneously, and thus creates widespread recognition. Often these people initially appear on game shows or reality TV shows. Can you name anyone who's been elevated to the status of celebrity via this route?

Today, television shows like *Entertainment Tonight* or channels like E! focus entirely on celebrity lives. Television made celebrity images available in ways the newspaper couldn't. The Web continues this trend in communication development. It offers additional access to celebrity that these other media weren't able to perform. With the Web, we can entertain ourselves more so than before by completely fetishizing celebrity status.

Elvis

One figure worth examining as a test case of celebrity is Elvis Presley. Elvis Presley's image in American culture revolves around both the concept of cool and the idea of the fetish. In his book *Mystery Train*, music critic Greil Marcus states, "Elvis had the nuance of cool down pat—the pink pants-and-shirt outfit he wore to his audition, the carelessness of his swagger, or the sneer around the edges of his smile—because the will to create himself, to matter, was so intense and so clear." Marcus represents Elvis' embodiment of cool as a place of individuality; i.e., Elvis' ability to create his own image. Typically, definitions of cool figures apply this trait to celebrities as diverse as Oprah Winfrey, Kurt Cobain, Lauryn Hill, and Bill Clinton. Closer examination, however, often reveals that media exposure shapes image more than individual will. How media portray the celebrity (good, bad, sexy, dull) contributes significantly to popular perception. With Elvis, television played a key role in creating his image by fetishizing his image to a national audience.

Elvis didn't command widespread American attention until he appeared on the *Ed Sullivan Show* in 1956. In what has since become a famous moment of censorship, the show's producers showed Elvis only from the waist up, afraid that his gyrating hips were too sensational for a national audience and 1950s values. Even without displaying Elvis' hips, television exposed Elvis to millions of viewers, who still interpreted this waist-up image of a shaking singer as sexual. Viewers didn't need to see his hips; the insinuated image of Elvis gyrating (by watching his shoulders and head shake) proved ample evidence of his sexuality. In addition, debate over the network's decision not to shoot Elvis' hips created an even more tantalizing image of the singer. What we can't see or read we often interpret as forbidden. Forbidden images are enticing. They ask us to imagine a situation or picture, and the imagination fulfills all kinds of expectations and hopes. In this sense, not showing Elvis' hips presented Elvis as cool from a McLuhan definition. Viewers compensated for the lack of image by mentally filling it in on their own. Television served several roles, therefore, in creating Elvis' celebrity image:

- It distributed his image to a larger audience than he could have ever achieved by touring the country and giving concerts.
- It presented Elvis as a sexual figure not by showing Elvis' sexuality, but by *not* showing it.
- By linking Elvis with a sexual image, it fetishized the singer for millions of viewers simultaneously.

Combined, these items presented Elvis as a sexualized celebrity. After Elvis' television appearance, he could be marketed to teenage girls as a fetishized object, a place for young girls to displace their emotions while purchasing Elvis memorabilia.

> You may not be all that familiar with Elvis. Come up with contemporary examples who you feel are analogous to Elvis (Nelly? Missy Elliott? Kurt Cobain? Michael Jackson? Madonna?).

As we've seen throughout this book, the cool image famous people become associated with is never an independent creation, but rather it is a market and technological construction. Elvis' sexuality became a marketing tool to sell Elvis' image. The Greil Marcus quote we began with describes the Elvis image most often marketed. The other Elvis image, which covers the end of his life—overweight, a Vegas performer, obsessed, forgetting the lyrics to his songs—is left out of this marketing strategy because it doesn't display Elvis as cool. Marcus' perception of Elvis, then, derives from technology's role in creating celebrity images. We remember Elvis as cool because of the various media replications of this image.

Technology gives us unparalleled access to the details of celebrity lives, but does it do more? Does it change celebrities into something other than people? Returning to our discussion of McLuhan's work once again, we remember McLuhan's assertion that cool media create high participation. If we follow this reasoning, we can say that our involvement in celebrity lives is itself a cool activity. In addition to tabloids, television shows, and entertainment-based Web sites, how else does technology expose us to celebrities?

Dead Elvis

In order to address this last question, let's return once again to the Elvis example. Greil Marcus extends his fascination with Elvis in another book, *Dead Elvis*. *Dead Elvis* is not a biography of Elvis; instead it chronicles the various places the image of Elvis or a reference to Elvis appears. Marcus studies media forms, such as speeches, advertisements, books, films, TV shows, songs, and consumer products, searching for Elvis appearances. Each medium produces an image of Elvis, but not Elvis himself. For example, artist Joni Mabe constructs collages of Elvis that juxtapose her personal confessions with the singer's image. Elsewhere, Marcus discovers a radio show, *Breakfast with Elvis*, in which callers phone in menus they would like Elvis to eat (even though he's been dead for several years). While Elvis the person is dead, his image lives on in these references in ways that are very different from the real-life individual.

Marcus observes that eventually, when we view all of these references at once, Elvis' image becomes so distorted that it no longer refers to the real live person who sang rock and roll and lived in Memphis, Tennessee, but rather to an ideal or concept that can be manipulated as desired. When the president's press secretary begins a talk by playing an Elvis recording or when a comic book parodies Elvis as a governmental drug agent, Marcus notes how each instance uses Elvis to produce its own type of meaning contexualized for its specific situation. In the end, Marcus collects a vast amount of material. Juxtaposed together, these numerous references produce a kind of language constructed out of celebrity image. Elvis may have died in 1977, but through technology and through mass media replication and distribution his image continues on. Marcus argues that we communicate via figures like Elvis and construct, in a sense, celebrity discourse to make sense of ourselves and our surroundings. Consequently, Elvis functions as a form of writing; his image is used for communicative purposes.

Dead Elvis asks an important question about our overall relationships to celebrity. What happens when celebrity images become language? The abundance of Elvis citations leads Marcus to theorize a celebrity language constructed out of textual and visual references to the king of rock and roll. Following Marcus' reasoning, Elvis is like the alphabet. To create meaning out of Elvis, we should treat these references as letters of the alphabet that, when put together, form ideas.

In your English classes, no doubt you have been schooled to see grammar as alphabetical. You might even remember the metonymic games elementary school classes play to remember the letters of the alphabet: A is for apple, D is for dog. Added to this structuring of language there exist numerous rules for syntax, spelling, and punctuation. But does the propagation of cool figures in the cultural lexicon produce a similar result? Can we say that there exist grammatical rules for fashioning ideas out of celebrity images? What might they be? Think back to our earlier discussion of Apple computers' "Think Different" billboards, which the Billboard Liberation Front defaced. How was Apple applying celebrity image to create meaning? Or let's return to the Nike Web site featuring Jason Williams' image. Is there a grammar to this kind of iconic display?

- Are there other celebrity images as dominant as Elvis'?
- Who might they be? Where do their images appear?
- If celebrities can produce a grammar of meaning, how might we write an essay using only celebrity references? What kind of meanings might such an essay produce?

Further Reading

Bolter, Jay David. "Identity." *Unspun: Key Concepts for Understanding the World Wide Web.* Ed. Thomas Swiss. New York: New York University Press, 2000.
Marcus, Greil. *Dead Elvis.* Cambridge, MA-Harvard University Press, 1991.
———. *Mystery Train.* New York: Plume, 1990.
Rojek, Chris. *Celebrity.* London: Reaktion Books, 2001.

Web Site

On this book's Web site you'll find a number of visual examples of how celebrity and the Web come together in strange ways. Take a look at these examples and the Web site's suggestions for comparing them with personal home pages.

Class Discussion

1. Discuss the differences and similarities between home pages, tabloids, and television in creating celebrity. Do these forms borrow from one another? How? Do we want home pages to replace the tabloid? Why or why not?
2. Similar questions are: Do our own home pages ever become tabloids? If so, how?
3. Why do we need celebrities? What is the purpose of fetishizing people we don't know?
4. Do you have a fetish? What is it? What or whom do you fetishize?
5. We've discussed several forms of technology that proliferate celebrity images; can you think of others?

Exercises

1. *I'm a Celebrity.* Go to the Web site for this book and read about how to set up a Weblog. Once you have it set up, create a space where you advertise yourself.

   In order to do this assignment, you'll first have to study other Weblogs and see how each, in a way, advertises its writer. For your advertisement, you'll need to promote your interests, ideas, concerns, etc. Use hyperlinks in order to do so. Find places on the Web like metafilter.com or bloggrolling.com where you can advertise your Weblog for other readers to find it.

2. *Fetish Page.* Create a Web site that fetishizes an object dear to you. You can choose an object from popular culture, a personal object (toy, clothing, memento), or celebrity. The purpose of this assignment is to demonstrate the rhetoric of fetishizing objects and people. Use hyperlinks and images in order to do so.

3. *The Dead Elvis Assignment.* Because Marcus' claim about Elvis seems provocative, we should test its validity. For this assignment, you will attempt to repeat Marcus' work on Elvis. Instead of focusing on Elvis, however, you will pick a different popular culture figure.

Pick a figure from history, movies, TV, music, sports, or some other medium. But make sure you pick a figure with a considerable amount of history behind him/her. Research this figure by searching for visual and textual references to either the figure's image or name. Use your library and the Internet for research, but also use unconventional sources: toy stores, tabloids, billboards, advertisements, consumer goods, etc. that might make references to your figure. eBay is often a good place to find these types of images.

Collect these references.

Construct a Web site that presents this figure as a collage through the various references you've found. You don't need to explain the connections. Your usage of hyperlinks and images should demonstrate how your figure functions as a form of discourse.

INDEX